THE TORONTO BLUE JAYS

THE TORONTO BLUE JAYS

Peter C. Bjarkman

B. Mitchell

This book is fondly dedicated to
TONY FORMO,
SABR's true computer whiz and Canada's number one Jays fan.

Cover design approved by loyal fans and bookstore staff of W.H. Smith.

This edition published by
W H Smith Publishers, Canada.

Produced by
Bison Books Ltd.
Kimbolton House
117A Fulham Road
London SW3 6RL

ISBN 0-88665-645-1

Printed in Hong Kong

Page 1: *First baseman Willie Upshaw and second baseman Alfredo Griffin strike a defensive posture in Exhibition Stadium in the early eighties.*

Page 2: *George Bell supplies power as he makes contact with a Mike Jeffcoat pitch in Arlington Stadium against the rival Texas Rangers.*

Page 3: *A rare SkyDome roof shot provides a unique perspective as veteran catcher Ernie Whitt bats against the Minnesota Twins in early September 1989.*

Below: *Another spring season begins as Tom Henke (far right) leads the Blue Jays pitchers in wind sprints at the ball club's Dunedin training facilities.*

PICTURE CREDITS

Action Photographics: 34(left)
Gary Hershorn: 11.
Hockey Hall of Fame, Toronto: 66(bottom right).
National Baseball Library, Cooperstown, NY: 20
Ponzini Photography: 6-7(all four), 9(bottom), 14, 16, 27(right), 32, 34(right), 36, 37(top), 52(both), 58, 59, 61, 65(both), 66(top left), 67, 70, 72.
Stock Market, Toronto: Dougal Bichan: 3, 49(bottom). The Hill Brothers: 12(bottom). Garry Lay: 22(top). Moore Photography: 15(bottom), 54. Derek Trask Ltd: 1, 15(top), 35, 39(top), 53, 57(bottom), 76, 77.
Topps Baseball Cards: 10, 18(bottom right), 22(bottom), 26, 64(bottom).
Toronto Star Syndicate: 23, 27(left [Jim Russell]), 55.
TV Sports Mailbag, Inc: 24, 25(both), 42(right), 47(bottom), 56(both), 60.
UPI/Bettmann Newsphotos: 2, 4-5, 8, 9(top), 12(top), 13, 17, 19, 21(top), 28-29(all four), 30, 31(both), 33, 37(bottom), 38, 39(bottom), 40-41(both), 42(left), 43, 44, 45, 46, 47(top), 50, 51, 57(top), 62, 63, 64(top), 68-69, 71, 73, 74, 74-75.
Ronnie B. Wilbur: 48, 49(top).

ACKNOWLEDGEMENTS

The author and publisher would like to thank the following people who have helped in the preparation of this book: Barbara Thrasher, who edited it; Don Longabucco, who designed it; Rita Longabucco, who did the picture research; and Elizabeth McCarthy, who prepared the index.

Contents

Preface

Below left: *One of the most popular of Blue Jays players, Kelly Gruber has become a mainstay at third base over the past three seasons.*

Below center: *Before his departure to the New York Yankees in early season 1989, Jesse Barfield was one third of the best outfield in baseball.*

Below right: *Lloyd Moseby has patrolled center field for the Blue Jays since 1982, and remains the club's all-time leader in games, at-bats, runs scored and hits. Lloyd is also one of the speedier flychasers in baseball today.*

Travelling from their recent beginnings to an American League powerhouse in less than a decade, Toronto's Blue Jays can only be described as a success story. Loaded with talented and colorful young players and blessed with baseball's most lavish pleasure dome stadium, the Blue Jays are one of the premier drawing cards of North America's favorite pastime. During the 1989 season over 3.3 million fans crammed into Toronto's Exhibition Stadium and passed through the portals of the remarkable Toronto SkyDome, establishing the largest home attendance total in the long, storied history of American League baseball.

Little more than a dozen years old, the Blue Jay franchise is largely devoid of the history and tradition that is the lifeblood of baseball legend and lore. Baseball teams, above all other professional sports franchises, bind together generations of sporting fans with the nostalgia of past seasons remembered. It is with the vivid, living memories of baseball summers past that most baseball fans fuel their passion for the game. For most true baseball fans, therefore, it is the storied franchises boasting decades of legendary accomplishment – the Yankees, Red Sox, Cubs, Tigers, Brooklyn Dodgers – that provide the richest baseball repast. Without such historical tradition a baseball team seems somehow devoid of the very substance that elevates baseball to its unique position, especially among our writers and intellectuals, as the nation's most literary and most mythic of sports.

What is there, then, about the newborn Toronto Blue Jays team – a team that has no Hall of Famers, no legendary diamond heroes of past decades and no past World Series glories to boast – that creates such a frenzied following? The answer, of course, is that Toronto's short yet dramatic dozen years of American League play enfold improbable and drama-filled events that supply some of the most thrilling moments of recent baseball history. This is a team that has played in two of baseball's most unusual ballparks and has experienced

Willie Upshaw strikes a patented pose at first base during spring training play. Sandwiched between such slugging first sackers as big John Mayberry of the late 1970s and Freddie McGriff of the late 1980s, Upshaw was the regular at first base between 1982 and 1987. Willie enjoyed a career year in 1983 – batting .306 in 160 games, and leading the ball club in four offensive categories by garnering 177 hits, belting out 27 homers, and driving home 104 runs. Upshaw closed out his big-league career with Cleveland in 1988 before playing professionally in Japan during 1989.

some of the most unorthodox on-field events in recent memory. It is also a team that has risen from abject baseball poverty to pennant riches in a shorter span than any post-expansion-era ball club, save the legendary New York Mets of the late 1960s. There is much, in fact, that links the Mets and the Blue Jays together as exemplary models of two of baseball's most successful franchises during the present baseball generation. Perhaps no other team from the golden age of televised baseball has been blessed with such sound front-office management and long-range planning as the Blue Jays organization under the tutelage of Baseball Operations Director Pat Gillick. None has developed a more productive farm system or has so efficiently exploited the new fountainhead of Latin American player talent. And none has more effectively marketed its team to hometown fans or created a more rapid and loyal national baseball following.

The story of the Blue Jays is also the story of colorful baseball personalities, from temperamental superstars like George Bell and Dave Stieb to incorrigible baseball clowns like outfielder Rick Bosetti, and undistinguished but colorful journeymen like Roy Howell (who never

Above: *The most savvy and dependable left-hander in Blue Jays history, Jimmy Key is here seen delivering his fastball in game three action of the 1989 ALCS at the SkyDome, versus Oakland's Athletics. Key won 17 games in 1987 but then slipped to rather disappointing seasons of 12-5 and 13-14 when he was plagued by arm injuries in 1988 and 1989.*

wore uniform shirt sleeves despite the often frigid conditions of Exhibition Stadium) and slugging, all-thumbs catcher Cliff Johnson. In the early days of the 1970s the Jays were one of baseball's most awful teams, losing 207 games in their first two seasons of big league play. By the mid-1980s they were a talented bunch of underachievers who couldn't seem to learn how to win the big games, blowing the 1987 division title with seven consecutive losses at season's end. By the close of the 1989 season they appeared to be a team that had finally lived up to its fans' long-harbored expectations, and done so with a dramatic flair for come-from-behind victories and nearly flawless home-field play.

The following pages replay the excitement of two recent dramatic American League pennant triumphs, along with the exasperating disappointments that shadowed the Toronto seasons of 1986 through 1988. Unabashed joys of expansion baseball are recounted here, and colorful baseball characters enliven the story of hapless early Toronto teams battling gamely against both nature's elements and the American League during the first decade of play in makeshift Exhibition Stadium. And finally, the embellished tale dramatically unfolds of two of baseball's most unusual stadiums, one a much-maligned baseball anomaly, the other projected as the first of a new generation of super-plush, space-age sporting arenas. In the several short but eventful summers of Toronto Blue Jays baseball, the newest Canadian ball club has been painstakingly built into one of the most colorful and successful franchises in baseball – perhaps in all sports.

Left: *1989 playoff action here features Jays second baseman Nelson Liriano tagging out sliding Oakland slugger Jose Canseco in the first ALCS game played at Toronto's SkyDome.*

Below: *The Terminator – Tom Henke – one of the most feared short relief specialists in the American League, delivers a hard one during ninth-inning action of the 1987 All-Star game in Oakland. Henke registered 86 saves over three seasons between 1986 and 1988.*

1. Okay, Blue Jays! From Worst to First in a Decade

The problem is that you acquire a past. In the beginning, what needs to be done is so clear, so obvious. When you have no players you must acquire the young players that you can find. When they are ready you put them in the lineup because the people who were there before them are just a holding action, just waiting until the future is warm. When you have no past you have no loyalties, no debts. You know exactly where you are in the cycle. You have a memory of no yesterday's dreams which still might flower tomorrow, and thus there is no confusion of tomorrow with yesterday, plans with dreams, or what is right with what is best for the team. On September 20th of 1987 the Toronto Blue Jays had a clean slate. They never will again. – Bill James, from The Bill James Baseball Abstract 1988.

A baseball team doesn't have to be ancient to exude a sense of baseball tradition. It doesn't require decades of pennants won and lost to mold a big-league team's colorful identity and its own rich sense of mythology. Baseball's foremost poet, Roger Angell, has embellished this theme while describing one of his own cherished teams – the New York Mets in their first hapless National League years. Born in 1962, the Mets were quick to develop an almost instantaneous and unrivalled baseball mythology, one arising from astonishing ineptitude (120 losses in their maiden season) and further heightened by legendary players who were already tied forever to New York's rich baseball past – Duke Snider and Gil Hodges of Brooklyn Dodger fame, and especially Casey Stengel of the glorious New York Yankees.

Nor is an eventful diamond history any guarantee of true baseball tradition, as Angell again cogently observes about certain less-favored teams, such as the Mets' New York progenitors, the Los Angeles (nee Brooklyn) Dodgers. For nostalgic fans like Roger Angell – those steeped in baseball lore and enamored of historic, urban ballparks – the transplanted West Coast Dodgers are the classic baseball anathema, a team with little evident appreciation for their once-rich baseball heritage. Upon abandoning historic Ebbets Field and traditional East Coast roots, Walter O'Malley's Dodgers callously discarded the familiar "Dem Bums" trappings of Brooklyn, as well, in order to cultivate a freshly polished image of wholesome All-American virtue and West Coast prosperity. And something significant to baseball was somehow lost in the process.

Just as the lovable New York Mets (at least the Mets of the 1960s) contrast with the sterile Los Angeles Dodgers of the 1970s and 1980s, so do Toronto's fledgling Blue Jays contrast dramatically with their French Canadian rivals, the National League's Montreal Expos. For one thing, baseball history in Montreal is distinguished by all-too-few "flaky" yet lovable diamond personalities – Bill "Spaceman" Lee provides perhaps the only noteworthy

Far right: *Outfielder Rick Bosetti was one of the most colorful ballplayers in the expansion days of Toronto American League baseball, a crowd favorite whose inspired play often overshadowed average big-league talents. Toronto baseball historian Tony Formo credits Bosetti and his exciting brand of play with a major role in transforming Toronto from a home of uninformed and apathetic fans into a respectable major league city.* The Rick Bosetti Baseball Book *was a bestseller in Toronto in the expansion years and the first Blue Jays literary venture.*

exception. Nowhere else in baseball can stark contrasts between the colorful, tradition-laden ball club and the sterile expansion franchise be more dramatically showcased, in fact, than with Canada's two Johnny-come-lately entries into the major leagues.

In Toronto, for example, the bizarre baseball personality has been almost a franchise trademark since the first opening day of April 1977. Most memorable was Rick Bosetti, a talent-poor outfielder who made up in outrageous on-field behavior for his distinct lack of demonstrable diamond skills. Bosetti's greatest claim to fame in the immense literature of baseball popular culture, for example, is his selection by humorous baseball authors Bruce Nash and Allan Zullo for enshrinement in their "Baseball Hall of Shame" – as the feature piece of a chapter entitled "The Sorriest Role Models for America's Youth" (*The Baseball Hall of Shame*, Volume 2, 1986). Then there was briefly tenured third baseman Roy Howell, who distinguished himself by flaunting bare biceps on the most wintry Exhibition Stadium days rather than by slapping base hits with any regularity. While batting .270 in the most productive of his three Toronto seasons, Howell only further spiced his reputation for inconsistency with a club-record nine RBIs in a single 1977 game against New York, nearly a fifth of his total season's output of 44. By the end of the five-year expansion period of Blue Jay history there was also can't-miss prospect Lloyd Moseby, who sulked his way out of the hearts of Toronto fans over the years, yet once gained baseball immortality by stealing second, then first, then second again – all on a single, infamous, botched baserunning play. Finally there was Cliff Johnson, prototype designated hitter, who looked and hit for all the world like Paul Bunyan, yet also unfortunately fielded his part-time catcher and first baseman positions like an untrained lumberjack with the misfortunate curse of a pair of stone hands. These were among the principle actors who have assured that Toronto baseball would always be a top entertainment draw – though often, like life itself, a losing proposition – even in the worst of expansion years.

The Toronto Blue Jay story, like that of the fan-rich Mets, is a tale of miraculous and equally sudden transformation from

Above: *The natural hazards of early-season Canadian baseball are demonstrated in this rare shot of the first pitch of the opening day game at Exhibition Stadium on April 7, 1977. The Blue Jays pulled off a 7-3 victory against the Chicago White Sox before 40,404 thrilled but chilled fans in the frigid downtown Toronto ballpark.*

such "lovable losers" into one of baseball's premier pennant-contending teams. It is the story of a ball club that has from the outset captured the passions of a nation of Canadian sports fanatics for whom baseball was supposedly only a secondary sport, a team whose players have to a man become national sporting heroes, as well as symbols of community pride and rallying points for national optimism. Despite an embarrassing opening season total of just 54 victories in its maiden 1977 season, the Blue Jays attracted an unprecedented 1.7 million paying customers as fan enthusiasm never waned that year. Overnight this team was also to become as much of a marketing success as it was an on-field baseball failure, with $10 million in sales of souvenir toys and T-shirts reported during the earliest months of the team's first campaign. These Blue Jays were suddenly aloft and soaring far beyond the fondest hopes of Toronto baseball promoters, and the flight has yet to diminish, though 13 summers and autumns have now passed without a single World Series game to be played on Canadian soil.

The first indication of things to come was the miraculous pennant season in the summer of 1985. Coming off the team's first two winning seasons (with identical 89-73 records), yet still finishing a distant 15 games behind the runaway Detroit Tigers in 1984, the 1985 Blue Jays, under fourth-year manager Bobby Cox, had been given

Above: *Lloyd Moseby hits against New York in June 1985. Moseby entered the 1985 mid-season stretch confident that the Jays could overtake the Yankees in the AL East – after all, he reminded reporters, the NBA Lakers had finally beaten the Celtics, ending yet another of sport's apparent dynasties.*

Right: *A colorful panoramic view of Exhibition Stadium's covered left-field bleacher grandstand. Among its several unique features, the Ex was the only big-league park in which the cheapest seats provided the park's only covered shelter.*

only an outside chance to seriously contend. But the slugging outfield duo of George Bell and Jesse Barfield, the solid pitching rotation of Doyle Alexander, Dave Stieb and Jimmy Key, and the remarkable long-relief work of Dennis Lamp (11-0, 3.32 ERA), together proved too much for the talent-laden American League Eastern Division. A franchise-high 99 victories led the Jays to within a single game of the American League title, which was lost only after a disappointing collapse in the final three games of the ALCS playoffs against the Kansas City Royals, baseball's eventual 1985 World Champions. Nine short seasons of player development strategies and bold player personnel moves had made the Toronto club one of baseball's very best. It seemed that baseball's ultimate Grail, a World Series victory, was only a season or two away.

Yet all did not go as might have been expected in the flush of a 1985 division title. After 1985, in fact, the Jays were quick to develop a reputation as baseball's most overrated and disappointing team. The tenth anniversary 1986 summer proved the old adage about the difficulties of repeating; under new manager Jimy Williams the club started slow and never did get untracked, limping home in fourth place and never a serious contender. The slow start of 1986 was soon overshadowed by the total stall at the end of the 1987 campaign, when the earlier high-flying Jays blew a golden pennant opportunity despite winning 96 ball games and engaging in one of the greatest stretch runs, head-to-head with Detroit, in recent American League history. Injuries to key players like Tony Fernandez and Ernie Whitt did in the Toronto pennant hopes in the end and the Jays dropped their final seven games of the summer, including a pennant-deciding three-game series with the Tigers in the season's final week. It was a last-minute fold-up which rivaled those of the 1964 Phillies and the 1951 Dodgers, and it left the 1987 and 1988 Blue Jays teams reeling with self-doubt and internal team dissension. The success that had come so rapidly to Toronto baseball seemed just as rapidly to have gone up in an inexplicable cloud of smoke.

There were, of course, plenty of baseball thrills in Toronto during the summers of 1986, 1987 and 1988. In 1986 a young rookie submariner, Mark Eichhorn, won 14 games in relief and held opponents scoreless in 42 of his 69 appearances, recording an incredible 1.72 ERA and taking the *Sporting News* rookie Relief Pitcher of the Year honors. Jim Clancy and Dave Stieb became the club's first two career 100-game winners during this stretch. But more importantly, George Bell emerged as a true superstar by the end of the 1987 campaign. Bell was not only a consensus American League MVP choice that ill-fated season, but the Dominican Republic's new national hero also stroked 102 homers in three summers while knocking in 339 runs as well. And just as controversial and electrifying as Bell – both on the field and off – was star pitcher Dave Stieb. Often unpopular with the Toronto fans because of his outspoken manner and flamboyant ways, Stieb remains even less popular with most American League hitters. Although never a 20-game winner, the ace Toronto right-hander has been at times more dominant than any other current big-league pitcher save perhaps Nolan Ryan. Stieb flirted with three near no-hitters in one year alone, losing masterpieces on his final two starts of the 1988 campaign and once again in the early weeks of the 1989 season to boot. One can only imagine their celebrity status and national appeal if Bell or Stieb were play-

Below: *A collection of happy Blue Jays All-Stars – shortstop Tony Fernandez (left) and outfielders Jesse Barfield (right) and Lloyd Moseby – mug for the cameras at the Houston Astrodome during pre-game workouts. This candid gathering occurred just hours before the 1986 All-Star classic, eventually won 3-2 by the American Leaguers.*

ing for, say, George Steinbrenner's Yankees, or within the equally relentless media glare of Los Angeles or even Chicago.

This is the team as well that now features baseball's most fearsome long-ball hitter in Freddie McGriff. McGriff does not merely hit home runs (leading the American League in 1989 with 36), he simply launches them. McGriff slugged 20 homers in a mere 295 at-bats in his rookie year of 1987, then led the club with 34 his sophomore season. Among this number are some of the longest shots witnessed in years in several of the American League's most spacious parks. And alongside McGriff's potent lumber the most recent editions of the Blue Jays have boasted as well baseball's most electrifying glove man at shortstop. George Bell's Dominican countryman Tony Fernandez quietly set a major league record for shortstops in 1989, with only six errors throughout a full season of play. This surpasses the standard of seven fumbles previously held by Eddie Brinkman playing for the early 1970s Tigers. Unlike the banjo-hitting Ed Brinkman (.224 BA over 15 career seasons), Tony Fernandez is a solid contact hitter and a flashy defensive showman as well, cut far more in the mold of magical St. Louis defender Ozzie Smith. The debate in fact rages as to whether Smith or Fernandez is truly the best fielding shortstop in recent times – perhaps even the best ever to play the game.

Below: *Fred McGriff displays the batting stance that has come to terrify American League pitchers for the past several seasons. Slugging 90 homers in the past three summers, McGriff has become a premier left-handed power hitter in the junior circuit. Acquired by a steal from the New York Yankees in a mid-winter 1982 deal, Fred McGriff doesn't merely hit home runs; he launches some of the longest drives seen in AL ballparks since the days of Frank Howard and Mickey Mantle.*

And then there has been the hoopla of the new domed stadium – baseball's first true pleasure palace devoted to 21st-century baseball viewing. Upon its opening in early June of 1989, the SkyDome became as large an attraction for Canadian and American baseball fans as did the Blue Jays themselves. Fans flocked to Toronto throughout the second half of the 1989 season as they have long flocked to Chicago's Wrigley Field, as much to experience the ambiance and spectacle of a famed ballpark as to witness big-league play itself. Before the Jays had even clinched a second division title in September 1989, Toronto fans had already flooded the Blue Jays' officials with unprecedented requests for season ticket applications. Reportedly over 40,000 fans have already demanded such ticket considerations for upcoming seasons.

Finally, to cheer Toronto diehard fans from Etobicoke to Scarborough and on to Niagara, there was the vindication of earlier late-season collapses in previous years. Frequent August and September rallies, including the eighth-inning heroics of two final-weekend games with Baltimore, set the tone for complete eradication of past failures with the successes of the 1989 comeback pennant chase. The Toronto Blue Jay baseball story of 1989 was, of course, undeniably the arrival of Cito Gaston as the team's new leader and quiet clubhouse general. If Gaston had been – as was widely reported – a secondary managerial choice of Executive Vice-President and General Manager Pat Gillick, he had been almost an unwilling candidate in his own mind as well. Lou Piniella was widely rumored to be Gillick's preference to replace the fired Jimy Williams, but George Steinbrenner kept Piniella unavailable by holding him to the full remainder of his contract as Steinbrenner's personal advisor. Thus Cito Gaston arrived almost as a desperation move; yet once at the helm he worked to quickly evaporate any remnants of dissension and begrudging play from his charges. The Blue Jays came soaring to life by mid-season and charged down the stretch with a 71-48 record after mid-May, identical over that period to the season-long .710 percentage boasted by the 1989 Western Division champion Oakland A's.

Some old war horses who arrived by trade also filled a huge and telling gap for defensive outfield play and left-handed contact hitting. Mookie Wilson and Lee Mazzilli

Above: *Nestled at the foot of the downtown CN Tower, Toronto's new SkyDome Stadium – with its retractable roof, its Jumbotron video scoreboard, and its fieldview hotel suites – is indisputably the world's most advanced and luxurious sports stadium. The movable stadium roof is twice the height of that in the Minneapolis Metrodome, and the Jumbotron is more than three times larger than any comparable videoboard in existence.*

Left: *The official Blue Jays mascot leads fans in hardy cheers in Toronto.*

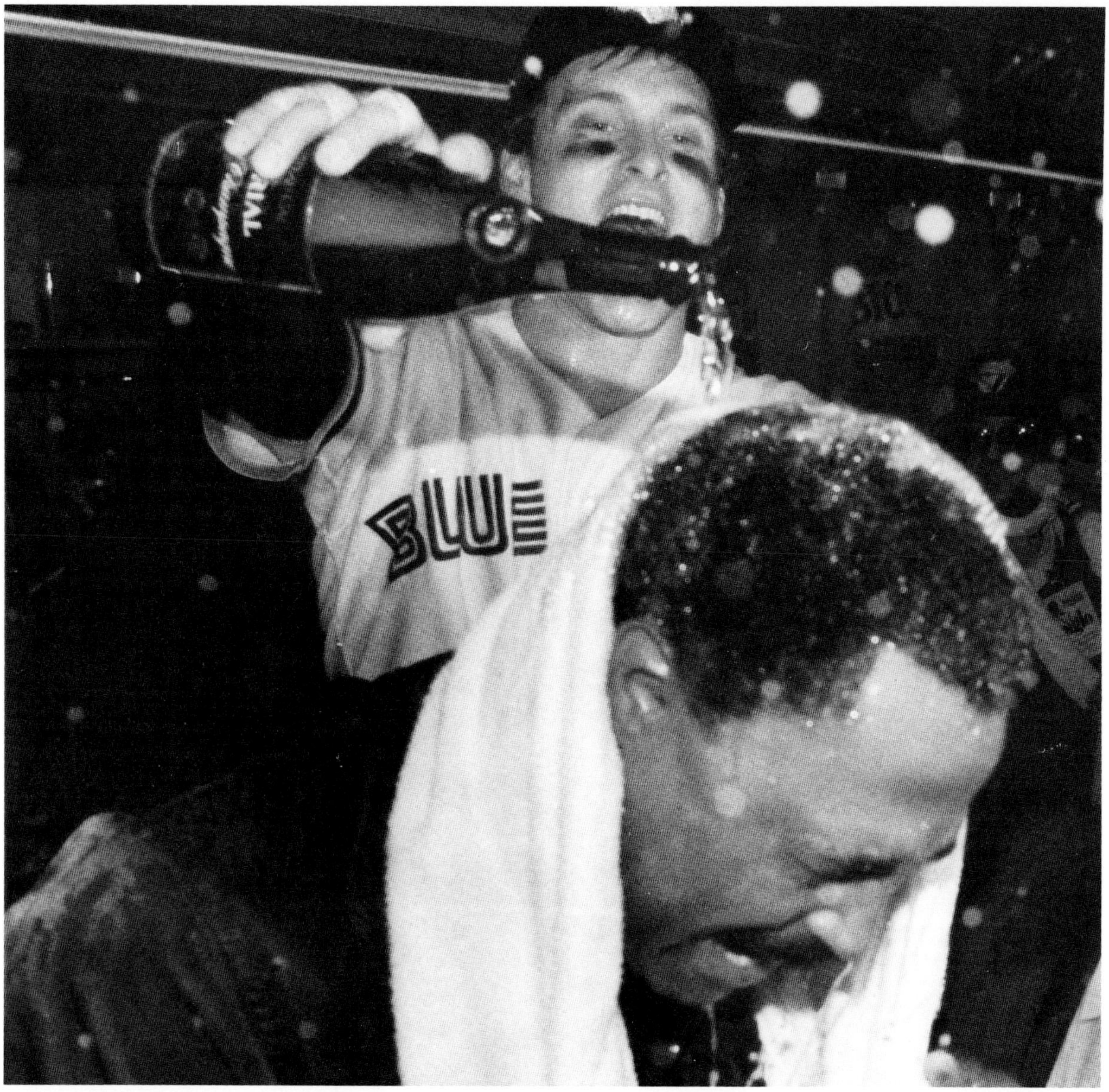

Opposite: *The surprise of the 1989 Toronto baseball season and early Rookie of the Year candidate was Dominican outfielder Junior Felix, a fleet flychaser with surprising power at the plate. Felix appeared with a bang in May, clubbing a homer on his first major league pitch.*

Left: *Manager Cito Gaston is doused with champagne by an exuberant Kelly Gruber in a locker room celebration of the Blue Jays' 1989 division title.*

also added an apparent clubhouse maturity and knowledge of winning. After their arrival the team improved from .500 to 19 games over in less than eight weeks. A final element in the revitalized 1989 Jays' championship season was, of course, the rookie year performance of Junior Felix. As a 24-year-old with only three years of professional experience, the diminutive Felix was not expected to advance beyond Triple-A Syracuse. But Barfield's departure and Ducey's failure to hit required another outfielder, and Felix arrived with a bang. While fading offensively after a July 30th shoulder injury, Junior Felix eventually dropped from Rookie of the Year contention. But nonetheless he was another surprise element in what proved a most surprising rebuilding 1989 campaign.

By the end of the exciting 1989 baseball season, the Toronto Blue Jays were established in only the third year of their second decade as one of baseball's most prosperous and entertaining franchises. Despite post-season playoff disappointments, the revitalized Jays of rookie manager Cito Gaston had at long last shaken from their collective backs a monkey that had taken hold during the dreadful final week of the 1987 pennant race. This was no longer a team of underachievers who seemingly couldn't win the big game when the chips were down and the pennant was on the line. Two dramatic eighth-inning comeback victories against the challenging Baltimore Orioles on the final weekend of the season had dispelled that myth for all time. Toronto's Jays were now a true American League powerhouse poised for further battle with the highest echelon of American League ball clubs – the young Baltimore Orioles, the always tenacious Boston Red Sox, the history-laden Yankees in New York and the ancient Tigers in Detroit. And with their new domed stadium and a season-ticket base of almost 30,000, the Jays were one of baseball's most lucrative business ventures as well. But it had not always been that way. In the chapters that follow the Toronto Blue Jays' story unfolds, from the earliest expansion blues to domination of one of baseball's toughest divisions.

2. Expansion Jays Aloft, With Talent in the Wings

The opening chapter of Toronto Blue Jay baseball ironically transpired far from the lush diamonds of summertime play. Official birth of Toronto's fledgling major league franchise took place instead amid much hoopla and formal ceremony in the elegant Terrace Ballroom of New York City's ancient Plaza Hotel. Such fashionable surroundings remind us that this great sport of baseball is, after all, a business venture, and that much of its significant history is played out in smoke-filled board rooms and across the high-finance bargaining table, between men more at home with a law book than a bat and glove.

The date in question was November 5, 1976, and the occasion brought together an august group of baseball dignitaries and officers from the American Leagues' two infant expansion ball clubs. American League Chairman Joe Cronin opened the morning's formal proceedings by presenting Toronto Blue Jay Board Chairman Howard Webster with an official certificate of membership valid for the league's seventy-sixth year of play. Comedian Danny Kaye, part-owner of the equally newborn and unchristened Seattle Mariner ball club, launched the true business agenda of the day – 12 rounds of the 1977 player expansion draft – by selecting journeyman outfielder Ruppert Jones as the first official Seattle Mariner. At exactly 10:31A.M. Toronto Vice-President and General Manager Peter Bavasi followed Danny Kaye to the rostrum to announce the choice of shortstop Bob Bailor, late of the Baltimore Orioles, as the Toronto Blue Jays' first drafted player. With the selection of this journeyman minor league outfielder from Connellsville, Pennsylvania – Bailor had played only 14 games in the big leagues in his two brief appearances with Baltimore – a second Canadian major league baseball franchise was a sudden and final reality.

Right: *Peter Bavasi served as Toronto's first Executive Vice-President and General Manager during the early expansion years and was clearly one of the early architects of later Blue Jays on-field successes.*

Above right: *Already a veteran of 14 big-league seasons, and possessing a lifetime 116-119 record when he came to the Jays via the expansion draft, Bill Singer was the opening day pitcher in April 1977 and thus threw the very first official league pitch in Blue Jays history.*

Over the next seven hours Bavasi and his staff selected an additional 29 players left unprotected by the existing 12 American League franchises – at a cost of $175,000 apiece. From this rare assemblage of failed veterans (such as Bill Singer of the Twins), not-too-promising youngsters (like lefty Dave Lemanczyk of the Tigers), and heretofore untested utility players (notably Jim Mason of the Yankees), an official major league roster was born. On paper the team looked at best like a mediocre entry in the Double-A Southern Association. But at long last Toronto was officially in the big leagues, and for Canadian baseball patrons, this was all that ultimately mattered.

The first Blue Jays' roster did not entirely materialize that day, however. Several players (Phil Roof, Dave Roberts, John Hilton, John Henry Scott) had actually been signed weeks earlier, having thus been employed by a baseball team which was yet unnamed and still in search of a field manager. Only Roof, who had played Triple-A baseball for Toronto's Maple Leafs 14 years earlier, and who most recently played for the White Sox, boasted previous major league experience. Perhaps the best prospects to emerge from the Jays' expansion draft windfall were only indirect products of the formal selections on draft day itself. Cleveland catcher Alan Ashby, for example, was acquired via an 11th-hour draft-day trade for veteran pitcher Al Fitzmorris (15-11 in 1976); and outfielder John Lowenstein and catcher Rick Cerone came on board the following month, also via Cleveland, for outfielder Rico Carty. The Dominican-born Carty, ironically, was later to return to the Jays from the Indians in time for two separate tours of duty during the 1978 and 1979 seasons. Other draft-day acquisitions who eventually saw more than modest playing time in a Toronto Blue Jays uniform were pitchers Jim Clancy, Jerry Garvin, Pete Vukovich, Jesse Jefferson and Mike Willis; outfielders Alvis Woods and Otto Velez; catcher Ernie Whitt, and opening day batting star Doug Ault. Only Clancy and Whitt became more than average ballplayers during subsequent seasons, however, and both were still wearing Blue Jay uniforms 12 years later at the close of the 1988 season.

Major League Draft Day of 1976 represented an exciting fulfillment for a nearly century-long dream of bringing major league baseball to the Queen City of Toronto. The true beginnings of the Toronto Blue Jay story stretch back much further than November 1976, encompassing nearly five years of active campaigning by city officials bent on gaining an expansion franchise, and capping nearly three-quarters of a century of vague hopes and often vain scheming for big-time baseball. Prior to the sudden and dramatic expansion events of early March 1976, Toronto had nearly landed a major league team at least twice before, each time seemingly reaching the portal of big-league baseball only to have the cherished prize snatched unexpectedly from its grasp. In fact Toronto had once earlier almost landed squarely in the National League, and had fate and politics taken a few different twists, today's Toronto fans might well have been loyal to the storied Giants, or perhaps even to the Johnny-come-lately Padres, rather than to the fledgling American League Blue Jays.

The city of Toronto had first harbored a dream of big league baseball as early as the 1880s, when Albert Goodwill Spalding reportedly visited the metropolis in mid-winter of 1886 and suggested that Toronto would be a most excellent site for a then-proposed National League franchise. Toronto was again prominently mentioned in 1899, during the time that Ban Johnson

Below: *Perhaps the strong tradition of Latin American ballplayers wearing the Toronto uniform could be said to begin with Rico Carty, selected from Cleveland in the expansion draft, traded back to the Indians before even a single Jays game was ever played, then reacquired by the Jays in time for the 1978 campaign. Rico Carty closed out the final two seasons of his illustrious big-league career in the Toronto uniform.*

Above: *Even at the turn of the century Ban Johnson, one of the creators and the eventual president of a fledgling American League, thought that Toronto would make a fine major league city. It would be nearly seven decades, however, before the pundits of America's favorite national sport would grant such status to their Canadian neighbors to the North.*

was scouting cities throughout the Northeast for his nascent American League, and also reported once again in 1919 as an almost certain entry for the never-to-materialize New Liberty major league. But it was not until 1973 that serious plans had emerged for expanding existing Canadian National Exhibition Stadium in hopes of capitalizing on yet new rumors of major league expansion. An often-repeated but perhaps only apocryphal story involves the reputed seeds of baseball's long-awaited migration northward to Ontario province. Metro (Toronto City) Chairman Paul Godfrey and Ontario Premier William Davis reputedly stood at midfield of Exhibition Stadium awaiting opening game ceremonies for the 1973 Grey Cup Football Game, and chatted informally about their shared dream of luring major league baseball into Ontario. An ardent baseball fan, Godfrey is reported to have whispered to Davis, "I think we should build a baseball stadium . . . right here." And in that single fateful moment what was to eventually prove the most momentous deal in Canadian sporting history was supposedly sealed – with little more than a handshake and a smile.

Two events which followed shortly on the heels of Chairman Godfrey's chat with Premier Davis in Exhibition Stadium were also highly significant to the eventual birth of the Toronto Blue Jays, albeit not before a convoluted series of events and misadventures. The first telling development was a commitment by the Metro and provincial governments to expand and refurbish Exhibition Stadium in order to accommodate a seating capacity of over 40,000, a necessary step in any plan to lure big-time baseball. The second involved promotion of 36-year-old Donald J. McDougall to the presidency of powerful Labatts Breweries, one of the province's leading industrial giants. McDougall was to prove a key figure in the subsequent ongoing political and financial maneuvering which lay behind eventually acquiring a big-league baseball team.

Over the course of the next three years the stadium was indeed rebuilt – albeit with taxpayers' money – though no probable team yet loomed on the horizon. During the same period McDougall joined forces with Robert Howard Webster, chairman of *The Globe and Mail* newspaper, to form an official consortium of Toronto investors, designed explicitly for the purpose of actively seeking an expansion baseball franchise. For nearly two years not a major league owners' meeting, World Series, or All-Star Game passed without a contingent headed by McDougall, Godfrey and Webster in attendance to promote Toronto as a potential major league city. Success seemed nearly at hand in January 1976 when the Labatts group tentatively reached an "agreement in principle" to purchase the financially troubled San Francisco Giants for a reported $13.5 million, but a court injunction launched by San Francisco mayor George Moscone delayed action just long enough for the entire deal to fall through by early March. Against this backdrop of blatant campaigns and backroom dealings other Toronto investors groups also entered the chase. As early as 1971, for example, before joining forces with the McDougall consortium, Montreal financier Robert Webster had himself made a first unsuccessful attempt to purchase and relocate the National League's faltering San Diego Padres, an effort which was repeated unsuccessfully in 1972 by McDougall as well.

The pursuit of the Giants had been a costly adventure for the Labatts consortium, and the group headed up by McDougall and Webster (along with the 10 percent partnership of the Canadian Imperial Bank of Commerce) had reportedly lost almost one-quarter million Canadian dollars in the first several years of their effort. After the aborted attempt to steal away the

Giants from San Francisco, things looked bleak indeed, and time for reflection and regrouping seemed to be at hand. Then – precisely when least expected – improbable good fortune suddenly struck. Just three weeks after the disappointing announcement that local San Francisco buyers had been arranged for the Giants, American League owners meeting in Tampa unpredictably voted 11-1 to expand to a 14-team circuit, and immediately announced preparations for offering expansion franchises to both Seattle on the West Coast and Toronto in the East. The entry fee was to be a tidy $7 million apiece.

Almost overnight, the wheels of baseball expansion began spinning wildly in Toronto. American League President Lee MacPhail – ignoring frantic overtures from several newly formed Canadian investors groups – appropriately turned to the solid McDougall-Webster consortium that had already been on the scene of expansion negotiations for more than five years. A last substantial hurdle had yet to be cleared, however, as Baseball Commissioner Bowie Kuhn pursued his own last-ditch efforts to delay American League expansion. Kuhn aimed to prompt National League club bosses to honor earlier commitments to the nation's capital by expanding into Toronto and Washington within the Senior Circuit. Nothing concrete was to come of this last-minute power play by Kuhn, however, and at long last the issue seemed settled. Ironically, the $7 million entry fee was little more than half the original proposed purchase price for the nearly moribund San Francisco Giants. This was a stroke of good fortune indeed for Toronto baseball folks, on more counts than one. Establishment of a brand new franchise not scheduled to compete until April 1977 promised sufficient diversion from the disastrous path of other recent expansion franchises. Such a lengthened time-frame would facilitate proper structuring of the big-league organization and allow adequate planning for a long-range baseball operation. In the end "Lady Luck" – the true patron saint of baseball – had finally smiled favorably upon the Queen City of Toronto.

While Metro government officials were busy allocating in excess of $2.8 million – decided by the lopsided vote of 27-3 – for further expansion and improvements on Exhibition Stadium, the new American League club began hiring its first payroll employees. Webster was named board chairman of Metro Baseball Ltd. (the official corporate franchise name), with Labatts Vice-President N.E. "Peter" Hardy pegged as vice-chairman. Peter Bavasi, 34-year-old vice-president and general manager of the San Diego Padres, was soon tabbed for a similar slot in Toronto. In what proved the first of many astute personnel decisions, the McDougall management team selected from the finest of baseball pedigrees in hiring Bavasi. The younger Bavasi was son of Padre president and ex-Dodger general manager, Buzzy Bavasi. Paul Beeston, a respected Ontario accountant, was lured aboard as vice-president for administration, while Howard Starkman was named public relations director, a slot he had long filled for hockey's Toronto Maple Leafs. Peter Bavasi himself demonstrated instant baseball savvy when he brought on board former associate Pat Gillick, then a New York Yankee farm director, as new VP for player personnel.

Left: *Pat Gillick, Executive Vice-President for Baseball Operations, is the true architect of the Blue Jays' sudden meteoric rise to the top of the American League East. The ball club's first player personnel director, Gillick deserves the primary credit for launching Toronto's extensive Latin American scouting and player development programs.*

Below: *Baseball Commissioner Bowie Kuhn campaigned for an arrangement which would have brought National League expansion to Washington and Toronto, Canada. Had Commissioner Kuhn won the day with big-league owners in 1976, Toronto might today be an NL city.*

Right: *A rare birds-eye view reveals the unconventional baseball dimensions of Toronto's Exhibition Stadium. Located on grounds of Exhibition Place – at the shores of Lake Ontario in downtown Toronto – the stadium stands within the 350-acre facilities of the Canadian National Exhibition grounds, the largest facility of its kind anywhere in the world.*

Below: *This Topps baseball card from 1977 displays the Jays' first manager, Roy Hartsfield, who lasted but three seasons.*

The most significant addition to the Blue Jay staff, of course, was Gillick. It was the 40-year-old ex-minor league pitcher who in short order became the primary architect – with an able assist from superscout Epy Guerrero – of a master plan of player recruitment unparalleled in the major leagues over the next 10 years. It was Gillick, of course – with his carefully fostered Latin American connections and his patient and astute handling of the Blue Jays' minor league program – to whom the lion's share of credit would soon be given for Toronto's remarkably rapid ascent directly to the top of the baseball world.

By November of 1976 one substantial element of a true major league team had already been put firmly in place – a roster of big-league players, albeit one stocked largely with minor league hopefuls and major league has-beens. A second piece of the puzzle had also been artfully constructed through selection of a stable team of administrative staffers and on-field management personnel. At the end of the team's first 12 years (by 1988), Webster, Gillick, Hardy and Starkman would still be sitting in their original management positions, with only Peter Bavasi having departed from the Blue Jays' front office team. Bavasi was to resign as president and chief operating office on November 24, 1981, replaced by Board Vice-Chairman Hardy. A third ingredient for major league play was the ballpark, a makeshift football stadium with plenty of character and an ideal downtown location, which was already undergoing final grooming for the 1977 opener.

What remained to be settled was only the most visible component of baseball identity – an official team name. In a move designed to boost both civic interest and community involvement, a "Name the Team" contest was held during June and July of 1976. This popular promotional event drew well over 30,000 individual entries and almost 4000 different and often off-beat team name suggestions. Proposed monikers included such memorable possibilities as Dingbats, Blue Bats, Hogtowners, Trilliums, Blue Sox, Bootleggers, and the inevitable Maple Leafs. Ten potential names were ultimately drawn randomly by a panel of select judges and "Blue Jays" was announced as the panel's popular choice on August 13, 1976. The winning team name had been submitted by no fewer than 154 different fans, necessitating a second random drawing for the promised pair of season tickets and announced all-expenses-paid trip to spring training 1977, which had been widely promoted as the chief contest prize.

The wealth of wild game birds inhabiting the Ontario region was perhaps motivation enough for the chosen nickname, although team ownership within the Labatts Breweries was more than likely doubly intrigued with the subtle reference as well to the company's popular malt – Labatts Blue. A team logo was promptly unveiled, which artfully combined team and company colors with identifiable features of the new Canadian franchise – bird head profile, baseball, and patriotic maple leaf underscoring Canadian national pride. In announcing the choice of name and logo, team officials boasted that "the Blue Jay is a North American bird, bright blue in color, with white undercovering and black necklace . . . strong, aggressive, inquisitive . . . it dares to take on all comers, yet is down-to-earth, gutsy, and good-looking." For die-hard Blue Jay fans the bird-on-baseball logo remains a point of unmatched public pride. To many state-side baseball fans, however, the Toronto insignia has been repeatedly judged one of the ugliest and least traditional logos ever to grace a big-league baseball cap.

Each big-league ball club seems to have its own distinctive date with destiny, a unique contract with the unpredictable and the bizarre. For the Toronto Blue Jays this stroke of repeated ill-fortune has from the first involved the saga and pageantry of baseball's Opening Day. The very first Blue Jays game ever scheduled, a spring training encounter with the New York Mets pencilled in for Grant Field, in Dunedin, unceremoniously and somewhat portentously fell victim to a soggy rain-out. But the drenching day that launched Toronto's first spring training gave little indication indeed of what lay in store for Toronto faithful less than a month later in Ontario.

American League Opening Day at Exhibition Stadium four weeks later proved equally as unfit for baseball play. Yet despite the anticipated bitter squalls of snow and arctic temperatures, April 7, 1977 remained a day destined for baseball immortality. The inaugural game in Toronto American League baseball history remains at present the most dramatic moment of franchise history. No team – perhaps in all of baseball's considerable history – has experienced such an eventful and even legendary opening game. Certainly none has witnessed such an Opening Day of high drama and memorable circumstance during the expansion era of the past three decades. The game-time temperature was an intolerable 32 degrees Fahrenheit, cold snow blew everywhere in the air, 44,649 fans (300 more than official capacity) remained on their feet and screamed continu-

Using bats as ski poles and catcher's pads as skis, a Chicago White Sox player treks across the snow-covered turf of Exhibition Stadium little more than an hour before the first frigid game was to launch American League play in the city of Toronto. A team of photographers scurries in the background to document what would prove one of the most bizarre scenes in the long history of major league baseball.

Doug Ault (1977-1978, 1980) will live on in the collective memory of Blue Jays fans for his opening day heroics of April 7, 1977. Yet like so many in baseball history who have achieved a moment of instant glory, Ault's big-league career never measured up to his dramatic debut. In four unspectacular seasons Ault would connect for only 15 more round-trippers and appear in only 256 games, achieving a disappointing .236 lifetime BA. But for one brief moment, Texas-born Douglas Reagan Ault was the toast of Toronto and all Canada as well.

ously through almost four hours of what only appeared to be recognizable as big-league baseball. Yet no one left before the final frigid out was made.

Authors Philippe van Rjndt and Pat Blednick have immortalized the moment in print: "What we bore witness to that afternoon had to be the most unbelievable spectacle in the history of major-league baseball: tens of thousands of parkas, overcoats, ski-jackets, sweaters and snow suits jammed up one against the other, elbows digging into ribs, lumberjack boots stomping on galoshes, eyes glaring out of ski masks as though this was a Montreal bank robbery. For a game that was traditionally southern, white and warm-weather, it certainly had come a long way!" (*Fungo Blues*, 1984).

Even before the opening pitch was launched, a deafening chant of "We Want Beer!" arose in unison throughout the park – a joyously playful outcry which would become a standard trademark of Toronto baseball for the nearly five years that preceded the first official ballpark beer sales at Exhibition Stadium in 1981. Richie Zisk of the visiting Chicago White Sox pounded out a two-run homer before most of the patrons were seated for the first inning, to stake the Chicagoans to a 2-0 lead, only to be answered by 27-year-old rookie Doug Ault in the home half of the first with a blast of his own deep into the bleachers in left. Opening Day in Toronto was destined to be the setting for historic home runs, and in the fifth inning rookie Alvis Woods of the Blue Jays became only the eleventh player in major league history to connect for a pinch homer in his very first big-league at bat. The final tally was a come-from-behind 9-5 victory for the home team, that left all 44,000-plus fans exhausted and thoroughly overjoyed.

Baseball has always been a game for individual heroes, a saga of men momentarily made larger than life by inspired performances upon the diamond. Thus the glory of opening day in Toronto fittingly belonged to just one man alone. He was one Douglas Reagan Ault, a journeyman infielder-outfielder from North Carolina whose career would already be over by 1980 and who would hit only 15 more big-league homers after his auspicious Toronto debut in Exhibition Stadium. Yet on April 7, 1977, Doug Ault was to find his own special encounter with baseball destiny. Again it is authors van Rjndt and Blednick who have immortalized the moment – a moment that a million or more Torontonians today falsely boast of having witnessed first-hand, ensconced in ski masks and battered by snow showers.

In the words of van Rjndt and Blednick: "Opening day, the first game, constitutes a pantheon just waiting for a hero to walk in. The man through the door was first baseman Doug Ault, who took one of Chicago starter Ken Brett's favorite pitches and laced it deep over the fence in left center . . . Because nobody expected it, the reaction rivalled the pandemonium generated by Moses' parting of the Red Sea. The bitter cold, the cached booze, the wailing kids, everything went out the window as 44,000 rose to their feet in an ovation that would have gone over well in Rome's Coliseum. It was *Triumph!* . . . You can still hear the screams and the cries, feel the pounding backslapping from total strangers – *Total Euphoria!*" (*Fungo Blues*, 1984). A second time Ault strode to the plate in the third inning and a second home run sealed Ault's place as Toronto's first and most indelible baseball legend.

The heroism of opening day was later to appear as a brief moment of inspired overconfidence, and for the first five years of their existence the Toronto Blue Jays never even threatened to win a pennant. For five years Toronto baseball featured a seemingly endless supply of promising rookies, career minor leaguers, players that nobody wanted – it was typical expansion baseball at its best (and its worst!), and often the most entertaining baseball of the team's first decade. The 1977 and 1978 seasons saw nearly identical numbers: 54-107 (45.5 games behind the champion Yankees) followed by 59-102 (40 games behind New York). Yet both seasons brought over a million fans pouring through the busy turnstiles (1,701,052 followed by 1,562,585) as baseball proved an immediate hit in this land of hockey.

The 1977 inaugural edition of the Blue Jays was surprisingly competitive for a ball club that finished with an unimpressive .335 won-lost percentage; 77 of its 161 games were decided by two runs or less. While Doug Ault became an immediate fan-favorite with his opening-day heroics, there were other colorful and tenacious performers as well: Otto Velez hit .422 the opening month of the season and was named AL Player of the Month for April 1977; Bob Bailor's .310 season average (496 at bats) was the highest BA ever for a first-year, expansion-club player; veteran Ron Fairly, in his twentieth major league season, became the first player since Stan Musial to appear in over 1000 games at both outfield and infield positions; and Dave Lemznczyk's 13 wins in 1977 was also a record for major league first-year expansion play. Outfielder Roy Howell enjoyed a single unparalleled day in late September as the hapless Jays rose up and thrashed the champion Yankees 19-3, with Howell driving home nine runs by himself, a mark that still stands today as the club's all-time standard. The return of Rico Carty from Cleveland (where he had been shipped less than a month following the expansion-day draft), along with the arrival of heavy-hit-

Below left: *Otto Yelez (1977-1982) was plucked in the expansion draft from New York, and hit 16 homers during the Jays' maiden season.*

Below: *Bob Bailor (1977-1980) earned fame as the very first Toronto draft pick in 1976. Bailor's .310 1977 BA remains a record for a player on a first-year expansion club, yet the injury-prone shortstop was destined to play out most of his 11-year career as a mere utility player with the Mets and Dodgers.*

John Mayberry (1978-1982), power-hitting first sacker who stroked 255 career homers with four big-league clubs, was the first Blue Jays slugger to smack 20 homers in a season (1978) and also the first to reach the 30-homer plateau (1980). Altogether Mayberry clubbed 92 homers in four-plus seasons in Toronto, still sixth on the all-time Blue Jays career list.

ting first baseman John Mayberry, formerly with Kansas City, also provided the Jays with some needed batting punch and with their first two 20 home run sluggers by the end of the summer in 1978.

The 1978 season also marked the arrival of rookies Rick Bosetti and Jim Clancy. The unpredictable Bosetti quickly proved to be a favorite, and the first of what was to become a seemingly endless parade of fleet, young, Toronto outfielders with moderate potential yet undistinguished yearly statistics both in the field and at the plate. Clancy was the only Blue Jay pitcher able to win as many as 10 games in the team's second year. But perhaps the two most portentous events of the Blue Jays' first two seasons occurred in the early summer of 1978, both actually transpiring far from the daily dramas being played out on the big-league diamond at Exhibition Stadium. The June free-agent draft that year found Toronto placed in the number two slot, where they selected a previously unheralded Oakland high school outfielder named Lloyd Moseby. Almost simultaneously, at the A-ball level, a struggling rookie slugger named Dave Stieb was being switched from outfield to the pitcher's mound in order to take full advantage of what seemed to be an uncommonly talented and lively young throwing arm.

On-field progress is not always either visibly steady or measurable to the average fan, and the 1979 season witnessed a number of apparent setbacks in the Jays' gradual march toward baseball respectability. The on-field record of 109 losses and 50.5 games out of first place was a franchise standard for futility, and the first phase of Blue Jay development came to an unceremonious end with the firing of manager Roy Hartsfield at the conclusion of the 1979 campaign. One pleasant surprise of the Jays' third year was the dramatic jump from A-ball to the majors by Dave Stieb, an unexpected event which transpired in early June of 1979. This talented rookie right-hander completed an outstanding 18-10 record (8-8 in Toronto) in a season split between A-level Dunedin, Triple-A Syracuse, and the parent club in Canada.

Under new manager Bob Mattick (elevated to the bench from his initial role as a scouting supervisor), the 1980 Jays improved to 67-95 (36 games out), the club's first season with under 100 losses. This certainly smacked of improvement, even if it was only good enough to register a fourth consecutive seventh-place finish. John Mayberry was the club's first 30-homer man that year, and future pitching aces Jim Clancy (13-16) and Dave Stieb (12-15) emerged as Toronto's most consistent hurlers. Stieb was a league All-Star selection in 1980 and also American League Player of the Month for April; Danny Ainge (later to star in basketball with the World Champion Boston Celtics) made a token appearance as utility infielder with 111 plate appearances; Ernie Whitt first took over as regular starting catcher, and Lloyd Moseby and Willie Upshaw caught on as regulars in the Blue Jay line-up by late in the 1980 campaign.

The summer of 1981 witnessed not only the most bizarre months of the first decade in Exhibition Stadium but also marked perhaps the strangest season in all of baseball history. An unpopular players' union strike nearly wiped out the entire summer's play and did succeed for nearly three months in obliterating daily baseball as North American fans had always known it. The split-season schedule format which resulted after resumption of play in mid-July was a laughingstock to baseball traditionalists (Cincinnati, with the season's best overall record, didn't even qualify for the revamped playoffs); yet this bizarre turn of events seemed somehow to signal an ironic improvement in Toronto baseball fortunes as well.

While the first half of the season had witnessed only further ignominy for Toronto (lowlighted by the major league's first perfect game in 13 seasons being thrown at the Blue Jays by journeyman Cleveland pitcher Len Barker on May 15), after the strike the rejuvenated Blue Jays of Bob Mattick managed to play .500 ball for all but the final two weeks of the season. Signs of change were everywhere apparent: Dave Stieb (11-10) became the Jays' first winning pitcher among starting hurlers; future superstar George Bell first appeared in the regular lineup during the post-strike month of August and responded with a .310 BA; and Lloyd Moseby tied for the club lead in RBIs (with John Mayberry) in his first full season of league play. The future of the Jays seemed to be arriving right on schedule, even if not everyone attending games in Exhibition Stadium was altogether aware of this in September of 1983. Even at Triple-A Syracuse the future was slowly stirring; there promising 19-year-old Dominican shortstop Tony Fernandez appeared on the scene by late season and drew immediate raves with his respectable .278 BA and impressive defensive range and agility.

The Blue Jays were never quite the same after the exotic split-season of 1981 – a year when Cincinnati's Pete Rose (well on his way to overtaking Ty Cobb as baseball's all-time base hits leader) did not garner his automatic 150 hits for the first time in almost two decades, and Montreal somehow emerged from the National League pack as Canada's first major league division winner. The season was full of surprises in Toronto as well, with the shortened schedule preventing a home attendance mark surpassing one million for the only time in franchise history; with Bob Mattick becoming the second Blue Jay manager to be rudely dismissed, despite his team's marked improvement; and with Bell, Barfield and Moseby starting in the outfield together for the first time on September 3 in Chicago. This latter trio was soon to be labelled by no less an authority than baseball statistics guru Bill James as perhaps the best all-around outfield trio of all time.

With the arrival of Bobby Cox as field manager on October 15, 1981, and the departure of GM Peter Bavasi from the front office little more than a month later, expansion baseball had seemingly come to an end and respectable big-league play appeared now to loom on the horizon for Toronto's big-league partisans. Some of the most colorful players and memorable events of franchise history had been the true legacy of the first half-decade of Blue Jay baseball in Toronto. Yet it was perhaps inevitable that the tensions of tightly contested pennant races would all-too-soon obliterate some of the unabashed fun at the ballpark which had so enlivened those maiden years for Toronto baseball.

Far left: *Dave Stieb has been the most consistent pitching star throughout the dozen years of Blue Jays baseball, pacing the club in career totals in wins (148), innings pitched (2458), strikeouts (1432), shutouts (28), and complete games (99). Making his major league debut in June 1979, Stieb's ten-year big-league career has been highlighted by three near-miss no-hit efforts, two of which came down to the game's final batter during consecutive starts in late 1988.*

Left: *Tony Fernandez debuted in Toronto at the age of 21 during 1983, following two seasons of .300 batting at AAA Syracuse. His continued hot hitting (.322 BA in 1987) combined with great range and a remarkable arm have made the Dominican youngster the best all-around shortstop in the big leagues, a yearly AL All-Star choice, and a leader in Toronto's two Eastern Division title seasons.*

3. The Sudden and Surprising Rise of Those Amazing Jays

Below: *After a cameo 60-game appearance during the strike-torn season of 1981, George Bell was plagued by injury and illness throughout much of the 1982 campaign, and did not reappear until mid-season 1983.*

Below right: *Doyle Alexander established a club mark (.639, 39-20) for career winning percentage.*

The summer of 1982 is best remembered as the season the Toronto Blue Jays finally escaped seventh place. And it all seemed to go according to some carefully executed master plan, as though plotted out with the ruthless precision of a corporate takeover or a measured military maneuver. Luck was there as well, of course – a late-season surge of 10 wins in the final 12 games and a corresponding collapse by the equally hapless Cleveland Indians allowed a sixth-place tie on the season's final day.

But all the elements had already been put neatly in place over the preceding five seasons, as corporate architect Pat Gillick was to explain in a recorded 1984 interview with authors Phillippe van Rjndt and Patrick Blednick. The Roy Hartsfield era had been a period, Gillick recounts, when winning was unimportant and the myopic goal was the stockpiling of as many young players as possible. ("We knew that whatever we did we would win no more than 50 or 60 games," Gillick remarked about those early expansion seasons.) Former scouting director and loyal organization man Bob Mattick had been brought in to manage the ball club during the next brief phase of team restructuring. Mattick was the ideal man for accelerated player development, with his intimate first-hand knowledge of the full core of young talent that had been carefully stockpiled between 1977 and

1979. ("That was his responsibility," recalled Gillick later, "to try to bring those players along, give them a good amount of instruction, more playing time than they actually deserved, so they could develop.")

As spring training camp opened for 1982 most of the youngsters and veterans alike seemed willing to echo catcher Ernie Whitt's assessment "that it was finally clear that we were headed somewhere." This new, upbeat attitude with which the Blue Jays seemed to approach the spring training routine in 1982 was clearly a reflection of the presence of new manager Bobby Cox. Changes in leadership during the off-season months signalled for just about everyone that the Toronto brain trust sensed a new phase of team evolution. Bob Mattick had gracefully announced his resignation on October 7, 1981, to become Executive Coordinator of Baseball Operations. A week before the first World Series pitch was thrown a replacement had been announced in Cox, former manager of the Atlanta Braves (1978-1981) and a man carefully chosen by Gillick as the perfect field leader for the final stages of a skillfully orchestrated organizational building program. A final front office changeover transpired that off-season as well, with Peter Bavasi, President and Chief Operating Officer, stepping down on November 24th, a move which further consolidated Pat Gillick's control over the full baseball operation. Hartsfield and Mattick had been mere caretakers, employed to build an expansion club and get the Jays off the ground. Now it was time to pursue a pennant in earnest, and Bobby Cox seemed the perfect baseball man for the job.

Like so many good managers, Bobby Cox had enjoyed only a most mediocre baseball playing career, one that saw a decade of dedicated minor league service capped by a mere "cup of coffee" in the big time and an altogether forgettable legacy of major league utility service. Almost lost to later events was the fact that Bobby Cox had been one of baseball's original bonus babies of the 1950s, receiving a $40,000 signing bonanza from the Los Angeles Dodgers as a promising schoolboy infielder in 1959. Cox labored through seven years in the Dodgers' farm system and through one additional year of minor league play for the Atlanta Braves before getting a brief shot with the Yankees in 1968 and 1969. In his two big-league appearances Bobby Cox played in only 220 games (135 in 1968) and compiled an undistinguished lifetime BA of

Below left: *Lloyd Moseby remains the only star player to be acquired by the Blue Jays through the free agent draft.*

Below: *Jim Gott won 21 games while losing 30 in his inaugural three big-league seasons.*

Fiery Blue Jays manager Bobby Cox here tucks his hands under his arms in a mock sign of mild restraint as he argues with home plate umpire Larry McCoy during Yankee Stadium action in 1984. The scene in this case rapidly escalated as Cox was soon ejected, yet had the final word by tossing several batting helmets from the dugout before departing for an unwanted early shower. Cox led the Jays to their first winning seasons in 1983 and 1984 and to their first-ever divisional title in the even more euphoric 1985 campaign.

.225. But by 1970 his tired knees were completely gone and Cox was unable to make the New York Yankees spring roster for the 1970 season. Gimpy legs had extinguished early a promising major league playing career.

But like so many semi-talented professional ballplayers who distinguish themselves far more by flat-out hustle than by raw natural talent, Cox had watched and learned carefully every aspect of the game. When his playing days ended, he was offered a managerial slot in the Yankees' chain and worked his way up to a valued position as big-league coach under Billy Martin in 1977, before landing his own first big-league managerial opportunity with Atlanta a season later.

The assigned role of new skipper Bobby Cox at the outset of the 1982 season was to begin trying to win – to get his troops to play like the future was now – and this was achieved in large part by assigning increasingly larger roles to promising young players. Willie Upshaw, for one, was ensconced at first base by the end of spring training as veteran John Mayberry was shipped to the Yankees, and the youthful Upshaw responded almost immediately with 21 home runs and 75 RBIs. Damaso

Garcia showed signs of future stardom at second with a .310 BA, an improvement of better than 50 points over his previous part-time season. Jesse Barfield, with only 25 1981 big-league games under his belt, was platooned in right-field and hit 18 homers while ranking second among American League outfielders in assists. And on the mound Dave Stieb further blossomed as one of the league's top young hurlers (17-14, 3.25 ERA). Jim Clancy rebounded from injuries, as well, with an impressive 16-14 record (3.71 ERA). Stockpiling talent under Hartsfield, teaching and developing young talent with Mattick, and turning the reins loose on a talented flock of youngsters under Bobby Cox – the Blue Jays had done it strictly by the book and had seemingly done it right.

Much of the excitement of the 1982 campaign was saved for the summer's waning weeks. Winning seven of the season's final eight contests, the Jays finished out at 78-84, the closest yet to .500 and good enough for a last-day tie with Cleveland for sixth place within the division. But the real fireworks came on the first evening of the final memorable 1982 homestand, in the seemingly meaningless first game of a doubleheader with struggling Minnesota. Making his second-to-last start in what had already been his most successful season, Blue Jay ace hurler Jim Clancy reached an improbable moment of near mound perfection. Clancy set down the first 24 Twin batters in order before seeing his dream of baseball immortality shattered when Minnesota designated hitter Randy Bush sliced a broken bat single past diving Jay shortstop Damaso Garcia. It was the fourth one-hitter in the Blue Jays' staff history (Dave Lemancyzk had authored the first in 1977), but the first in which the only safety had come within three outs or less of a perfect game effort. And until Dave Stieb's three bizarre encounters with pitching perfection during 1988 and 1989, this would remain for the rest of the decade the closest thing to a taste of no-hit immortality that a Toronto pitcher would be privileged to savor.

If any doubts remained among Toronto baseball watchers about Gillick's master plan, they were all but finally obliterated during the ensuing 1983 and 1984 seasons. For 1983 was the season when for the first time the Blue Jays had become serious pennant contenders. The on-field improvement was almost geometrical in its rapid progression – a fourth-place finish in 1983, but with a club-record 89 victories and only nine games behind the victorious Orioles (only three games behind second place Detroit and but two games out of third). May 29th of that year was a truly historic day in Toronto baseball as for the first time the Jays found themselves occupying first place. But while few fans today may remember the significance of that late May date, fewer still have forgotten another moment of Exhibition Stadium history played out later that August. It was August 4th and the heady Jays were on the verge of a possible four-game home sweep of the proud Yankees; but few remember much of what happened that day (the Yankees won the game 3-1) beyond the events surrounding Yankee outfielder Dave Winfield. Concluding between-inning warm-up tosses with a ball boy along the left-field line, Winfield scored a direct hit on the head of an unsuspecting seagull perched on the artificial turf, killing the unfortunate fowl instantly. Blue Jay front office personnel were soon embarrassed and Yankee management outraged when Winfield was arrested by local constables at game's end

Below left: *Willie Upshaw still ranks high in a number of career offensive categories: second in at-bats, doubles and runs scored; third in games played and triples; and fourth in total hits, total bases, and extra-base hits.*

Below: *Buck Martinez is today familiar to Blue Jays followers as a commentator on Toronto TV baseball broadcasts. Prior to his media career, the California native enjoyed a productive 17-year big-league catching career, the final six seasons in a back-up role with the Blue Jays. Buck Martinez is also a published author, penning two season-in-review books on the 1985 and 1986 Toronto campaigns.*

and formally charged with willful destruction of wildlife. Those charges were soon enough dropped by red-faced local officials, and Metro Chairman Paul Godfrey was even called upon to issue a public apology to the bemused New York outfielder.

Acquisition of Cliff Johnson (DH, Oakland), Jorge Orta (OF-DH, Mets) and Dave Collins (OF, Yankees) had solidified the young Toronto outfield during off-season dealing in the winter of 1982-1983. It was the dramatic improvement in the DH role, in fact, that had thrust Toronto into pennant contention in 1983. While in 1982 the Jays had ranked dead last in the 14-team circuit in DH production, a mere year later they ranked absolute first (with 34 homers and 113 RBIs). The final days of August saw the club still only one and a half games behind the leaders, and the Jays had in fact been tied for the division lead as late as July 25th. But pennant fever was dowsed quickly enough by a late-August string of heart-rending, extra-inning defeats. None was more heart-stopping than what transpired in Baltimore on the fateful night of August 24th, perhaps the most infamous mid-season moment in franchise history. Needing a victory to move within a half game of the pace-setting Orioles, the Jays had sailed into the ninth behind Jim Clancy with a secure 3-1 lead. Baltimore rallied for the tying runs in the bottom of the final frame and paid a seemingly heavy price for doing so. It seems as though Baltimore manager Joe Altobelli had outmaneuvered himself in the comeback attempt, running out of available catchers and now being faced with substituting diminutive second baseman Len Sakata in the unfamiliar backstop spot. Cliff Johnson connected for a solo homer to begin the tenth, and then three consecutive Blue Jays (Barry Bonnell, fleet Dave Collins, and nimble Willie Upshaw) reached first base – and to the astonishment of all in the ballpark, all three were promptly picked off first by Orioles left-hander Tippy Martinez. The key figure, shockingly, in this bizarre piece of baseball history was the novice catcher Sakata, whose very presence behind the plate had seduced all three overanxious baserunners into straying too far off the bag, and thus they fell easy prey to Martinez's snappy pickoff move. And Sakata, himself, was not done yet. He later slugged the three-run homer that sealed the Jays' defeat and broke the spirit of a young team that never fought its way back into the pennant race after that fateful night.

Perhaps the true key to the Jays' strong 1983 season showing, despite their late-season collapse, was stabilization of the youthful Blue Jay pitching staff. Stieb (17-12), Clancy (15-11) and Luis Leal (13-12) were again the core, and Doyle Alexander (7-6) was signed on as a free agent after being released by the Yankees in June, and supplied some much-needed late-season strength. And for added measure there was the emergence of Lloyd Moseby as one of the finest young outfielders in the game. Moseby was the first Blue Jay to score 100 runs in a single season, reaching that club milestone on September 19th. Willie Upshaw contributed in major fashion as well and was the first Toronto batsman to post 100 RBIs for a single campaign, reaching his own personal milestone the day after Moseby had reached the century mark in runs. Not to be outdone, Damaso Garcia batted over .300 for the second consecutive year, stealing 54 bases as well, second in the American League behind only Rickey Henderson's record-smashing 130 total.

April of 1984 brought a strange mix of joy and foreboding to the Queen City baseball scene. The Blue Jays – far sooner than either rabid fans or skeptical experts had ever expected – were no longer merely expansion laughingstocks. In what was admittedly baseball's best division, the 1983 Jays had found themselves firmly entrenched in the thick of pennant contention. Yet a pervasive sense of tragedy appeared to plague this young team, and by

Opposite: *Jesse Barfield heads for first after stroking another hit. Perhaps the most popular player ever to don a Toronto uniform before his departure to New York early in the 1989 campaign, Jesse is a superb outfielder who has won two Rawlings Golden Gloves for defensive excellence.*

Below: *DH Cliff Johnson strokes a double in 1985 game action against the Kansas City Royals.*

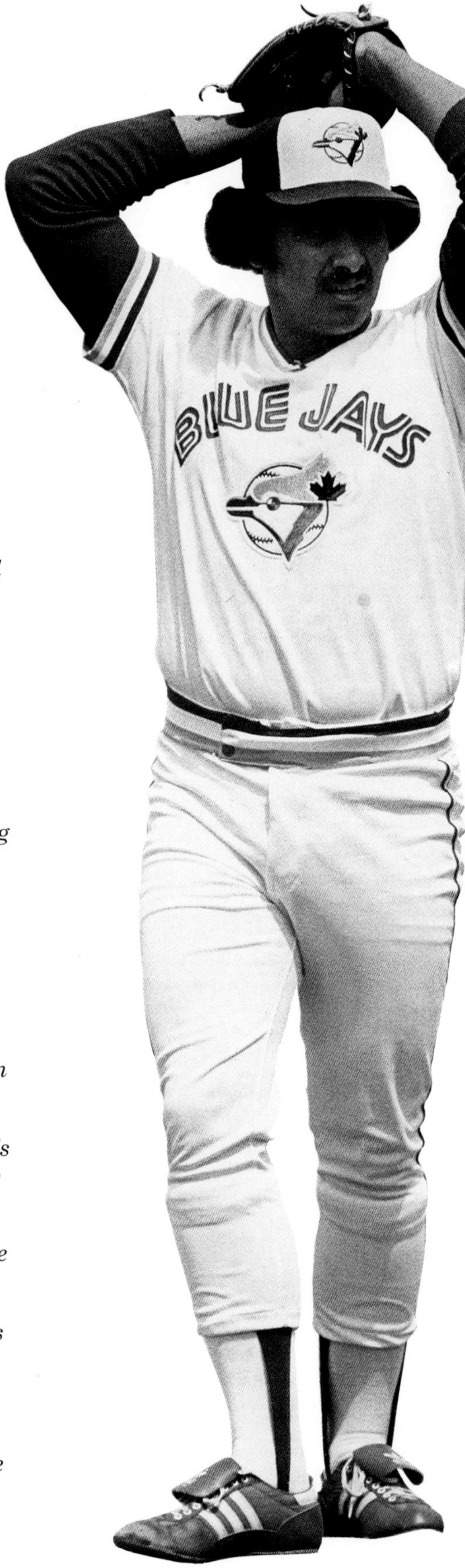

Right: *Venezuelan Luis Leal won 51 ball games for Toronto in a six-year career which began in 1980 and saw two seasons of 13 wins in 1983 and 1984. Leal did have the dubious honor of leading the American League in games lost (13) during the strike-shortened 1981 season.*

Far right: *Dennis Lamp enjoyed a sparkling 11-0 campaign during the title season of 1985, anchoring the bullpen staff with yeoman service in the middle relief role. But Lamp's big splash in Toronto undoubtedly had come in January of 1983, when he became the ball club's first significant free agent signing. The previous 1983 season he had recorded 15 saves for the Western Division champion Chicago White Sox, yet despite his 1985 success Lamp never became the dominant closer the Jays hoped for.*

the spring of 1984 it had become unsettlingly apparent that baseball fortunes for Toronto might not rest solely in the hands of front office wizards like Pat Gillick, nor even in the bats and gloves of stellar onfield performers like Barfield, Moseby and Bell. Other darker forces seemed at work, and one of those forces was residing to the east, in Detroit's Tiger Stadium.

By early 1984 the Jays had dramatically improved their most notable earlier weakness – the bullpen – with acquisition of the team's first significant free agent talent, relief ace Dennis Lamp, who had labored most recently for Chicago's White Sox and had earned 15 saves in 1983. Barry Bonnell had also been traded to Seattle in December of 1983 for left-hander Bryan Clark, another move designed to shore up a bullpen crew that had floundered for several years at the middle of the American League pack. Yet the bullpen still faltered in crucial game situations as the summer of 1984 progressed, and the Achilles heal of the team proved again to be their inability to save close, one-run games. Lamp's one great season was still a year away, and the expensive acquisition proved in 1984 to be little more than an ineffectual luxury, saving but nine games and losing as many (eight) as he won. Clark was simply awful, not saving a single game and being hammered for a club-worst 5.91 ERA (1-2 record) over a mere 46 innings of lackluster relief work. After winning a remarkable 19 consecutive one-run decisions in the first half of the season, the bullpen collapsed almost totally after the mid-season All-Star break. An embarrassing total of 25 losses in 40 one-run contests over the remainder of the schedule spelled certain demise for any lingering pennant hopes in the face of the Tiger's relentless year-long victory onslaught.

For it wasn't so much what the Jays did as what the Detroit Tigers had accom-

Above: *Fans queue up for precious last-minute game tickets outside of Exhibition Stadium. Between 2.1 and 2.8 million paying customers poured into anachronistic Exhibition Stadium in each of the Blue Jays' final five years in the old ballpark. Only the strike-torn and shortened 1981 season has seen the Toronto Blue Jays fail to draw at least one million paying home fans.*

plished in 1984 that made the difference. With an amazing 25-4 bolt from the gate, the Detroiters were already seven games ahead of the second-place Jays by May 11th, and never paused to look back at the rest of the league. Despite another 89-victory season, the Jays were, in fact, never even serious contenders after the opening two weeks of league play. The unstoppable Tigers won a record 38 of their first 49 decisions and Toronto – despite a more-than-respectable 34-16 mark (.680) – on June 4th was still no closer to the lead than four and a half games. Second place was something of a hollow consolation for a Blue Jays team that finished 15 games behind the leaders by season's end and never actually tasted the thick of the pennant race it had enjoyed in 1983. Yet there was a bright side as well. For the second straight season Bobby Cox had led his charges to 89 victories, and the Jays had finished five games better than the league's Western Division winner (Kansas City), possessing the third best record that year in all of baseball.

By the end of the 1984 season a second brief era in Blue Jay history seemed to have passed. For the first time the Jays had drawn more than two million fans into Exhibition Stadium, and by that standard alone they were now one of baseball's elite franchises. This was no longer a patsy expansion ball club doomed to be cannon fodder for all pennant contenders. But it was also no longer a team to be praised just for staying alive in a pennant race a week or two beyond mid-season's All-Star Game break. The Jays now seemed to have all the requisite pieces neatly in place for a serious pennant run, and fans and sportswriters were now picking the Jays to break through to the top with each new spring season. The time was at hand either to produce or to scrap the model and start over. In short, success had already spoiled the expansion Blue Jays, and Toronto baseball fans were already running surprisingly short of patience.

4. A Championship Season – The Year the East was Won

Below: *Jimmy Key remains the most successful and consistent lefty in club annals, posting a 74-49 career mark and ranking first on the club's career ERA list (3.36). Key also ranks third among all Toronto pitchers in career wins, total innings pitched and shutouts.*

For nearly every baseball franchise (save perhaps those in Seattle and Arlington) there comes sooner or later that one ultimate dream season, that fateful summer when everything falls suddenly into place and wildest dreams of glory and of victory fall dramatically within reach. In Philadelphia, or perhaps Chicago, fans may wait nearly five decades for such a season; in Toronto it came most miraculously after only eight short campaigns of American League play. The unstoppable Tigers of 1984 slumped badly in 1985 and the door was thrust wide open for Bobby Cox and his battling young Blue Jays. Tom Henke (13 saves) had emerged from the minors and Bill Caudill (14 saves) was plucked from free agency to at long last elevate the bullpen to the level of major league competency. Doyle Alexander (17-10) and newcomer Jimmy Key (14-6) supported veteran Dave Stieb (11-10) in the starting mound assignments, and Dennis Lamp enjoyed a remarkable 1985 campaign (11-0) in his familiar middle-relief role. This sudden wealth of pitching was bolstered with some of the league's best slugging – 28 home runs for Bell and 27 for Barfield, plus 95 RBIs by the former and 84 from the latter – and the Blue Jays were off and flying early in their best campaign to date.

The 1985 season brought hopes of new competitiveness and dramatic advancement in the league standings after the successes of the euphoric 1984 second-place season. This new confidence and expectation were increased by a couple of off-season trades that seemed to plug the one glaring weakness that had remained in what was otherwise beginning to look like a pennant-contending ball club. At the conclusion of the December 1984 winter meetings in Dallas it was announced that Toronto had acquired ace short reliever Bill Caudill from the Oakland Athletics for shortstop Alfredo Griffin and speedy outfielder Dave Collins. Within weeks, disappointing hurler Jim Gott was shipped west as well, this time to the San Francisco Giants in exchange for lefty reliever Gary Lavelle. While the free-spirited Caudill had saved an impressive 88 games for non-contending teams (Seattle as well as Oakland) over the previous three seasons, Lavelle was the Giants' all-time career saves leader with a string of 127. Together this duo promised to provide the one element so glaringly absent from the 1984 ball club and all previous editions of the Toronto Blue Jays as well – a dominating bullpen closer who could be counted on regularly to close down late-inning outbursts by potent enemy bats.

The Jays moved into first place to stay on May 13th and pennant euphoria ignited Exhibition Stadium throughout the remaining long summer months. The city responded in predictable fashion and a record 2,468,925 fans poured through the turnstiles for a second consecutive season over the two-million attendance figure. The players who carried the team most of the year were of course Bell and Barfield, though Rance Mullinicks (.295 BA with 108 hits) and Garth Iorg (.313 BA in 288 at bats) hit consistently in the clutch as well. Yet the newfound bullpen strength was indeed the catalyst for a dramatic improvement in the 1985 Blue Jays during the late-season stretch run. This was no longer a team that saw game after game slip away for inability to hold onto a slim late-inning lead.

While the load was not carried as exclusively as expected by newcomers Caudill and Lavelle, the two 1984 winter acquisitions did play a substantial role in rejuvenated team fortunes the following spring. Bill Caudill saved 14 games and maintained a sub-3.00 ERA before fading somewhat after mid-season. Lavelle saved only eight games, yet performed yeoman-like service with 73 innings pitched and 69 game appearances (besting Caudill by two as the club leader in this category). As Caudill tailed off in effectiveness, veteran Jim Acker took over the short relief situations and himself compiled substantial numbers (seven victories and ten saves in 61 game appearances and 86 innings pitched). Yet it was surprising rookie Tom Henke and third-year Blue Jay Dennis Lamp who ultimately pumped lifeblood into the Toronto pitching staff throughout late-season play. Lamp compiled a sterling 11-0 mark (3.32 ERA) and proved the most consistent hurler on the entire staff, appearing in both long and middle relief spots down the stretch. After being summoned from Syracuse in late July, however, Henke became the biggest story of the rejuvenated Toronto bullpen corps, registering 13 saves and a 2.03 ERA. It was "The Terminator" Henke who emerged the dominating late-inning closer that Gillick and his staff had hoped they might have snared in handing out a long-term, multi-million dollar contract to Bill Caudill the previous December. Caudill proved a distinct disappointment, as he would register only two more saves in 1986 before returning to Oakland. Henke, by contrast, would continue his blistering pace with a club-record 27 saves during the 1986 campaign.

In late summer it began to look as if pennant dreams might be a true reality for Toronto as the stubborn Jays never fell from their perch in first place after mid-May. Doyle Alexander anchored the starting pitching as he won 17 games for the second consecutive season. Dave Stieb compiled only 14 wins (against 13 losses) but was the league leader in ERA (2.48). And vastly improved Jimmy Key (14-6, 3.00 ERA) provided the first wins on the ball club by a left-handed starter since Paul Mirabella had defeated Boston in October of 1980. The aggregate Toronto bullpen enjoyed by far its best season ever (47 saves and a 35-20 winning record), and the difference this time around translated dramat-

Above: *Lefty hitter Rance Mulliniks supplies steady utility play at several infield positions, while providing a productive spare bat as well. Mulliniks hit .324 in 1984, .310 in 1987, and an even .300 in 1988.*

Left: *Steady second baseman Damaso Garcia completes a classic double-play throw to first as he leaps over the hard-sliding Bob Boone of the California Angels. The scene was at Exhibition Stadium during July of the 1985 title-winning season.*

Above: *Jesse Barfield here successfully stretches for the plate as Brewers catcher Dave Huppert vainly reaches for a tardy throw from infielder Randy Ready in Milwaukee. The date was September 29, 1985, only days before the Blue Jays clinched their first-ever American League East division championship.*

ically into the league standings as well.

Nearly 47,000 crammed the "Big Bird Feeder" on Saturday afternoon, October 5th, as pennant fever reached epidemic proportions. The second-place Yankees of manager Billy Martin were in town and the pennant was still very much up for grabs; the Jays were nursing a two-game margin after a Friday night 4-3 loss to New York, and with but a scant two games to play. While weather conditions seemed to favor the Yankees – loaded with left-handed power and primed to exploit the prevailing right-field breeze against crafty right-hander Doyle Alexander – it was the Toronto bats instead which quickly exploited the stiff Lake Ontario winds. Ernie Whitt cracked a homer in the second and Lloyd Moseby and Willie Upshaw followed with back-to-back left-handed blasts in the bottom of the third. From that point on it was all Doyle Alexander, and no one in the huge home crowd was disappointed, as Alexander shut down the New Yorkers with a masterful 5-1 performance. The veteran hurler allowed only five scratch hits along the way, and most remarkably, not a single ball was stroked toward right field by the New Yorkers, who were unable to exploit the prevailing outfield winds.

For those who note such detail, it was exactly 4:28 P.M. on October 5th when George Bell squeezed Ron Hassey's lazy fly to left field for the final putout, and Toronto enjoyed its first-ever championship celebration. Only eight years, five months, twenty-eight days, and approximately three hours had passed since Bill Singer had flung the first expansion pitch past Ralph Garr to open play in Exhibition Stadium. Only the New York Mets, among baseball's expansion-era teams, had won a division or league title quicker (seven years), and no franchise in the American League had ever come close to the Jays' heady record for expansion-era championship success. To some it perhaps had seemed like an eternity, to others perhaps not more than a matter of days.

The pandemonium which surrounded clinching of Toronto's first division title provided a cherished moment of Canadian sporting history rivaled only by Doug Ault's heroics in the legendary opening game of April 1977. That the pennant race had come down to the season's final week only added a fitting touch of baseball drama in the finest poetic traditions of the national pastime. And this drama was still further heightened by the Jays' heartbreaking 4-3 10-inning loss the previous night of October 4th, before the second largest pre-SkyDome Toronto baseball crowd ever (47,686). But in less than 24 hours agony was replaced by ecstacy as Bell caught Hassey's harmless fly ball and the long-awaited celebration began.

In the immediate aftermath of a first-ever division title, the disappointing seven-game American League Championship Series defeat which followed, at the experienced hands of the western division Kansas City Royals – baseballs' eventual 1985 World Champions – seemed at the time to be almost anti-climactic. It was in this doomed series, however, that the Jays first earned the "hopeless losers" label that was to plague them throughout most of the second half of the decade. With home field advantage in the first seven-game series of ALCS history, the Jays seemed a strong bet to parlay division title play into Canada's first entry into fall World Series play as well. But it simply wasn't in the cards for the 1985 Toronto Blue Jays, though few would have guessed it after the first four games of the short championship series.

Above: *Veteran Doyle Alexander turned in four solid seasons for Toronto, winning 17 games twice, in 1984 and 1985. Now a Detroit Tiger, Alexander is rapidly approaching 200 career wins in his 20th full season.*

Left: *Much sooner than even the most optimistic fan could have hoped, the Blue Jays celebrate a division-clinching victory over the Yankees on October 5, 1985. Here jubilant teammates carry winning pitcher Doyle Alexander from the field, moments after George Bell caught the fly ball that sealed the New Yorkers' fate by the score of 5-1.*

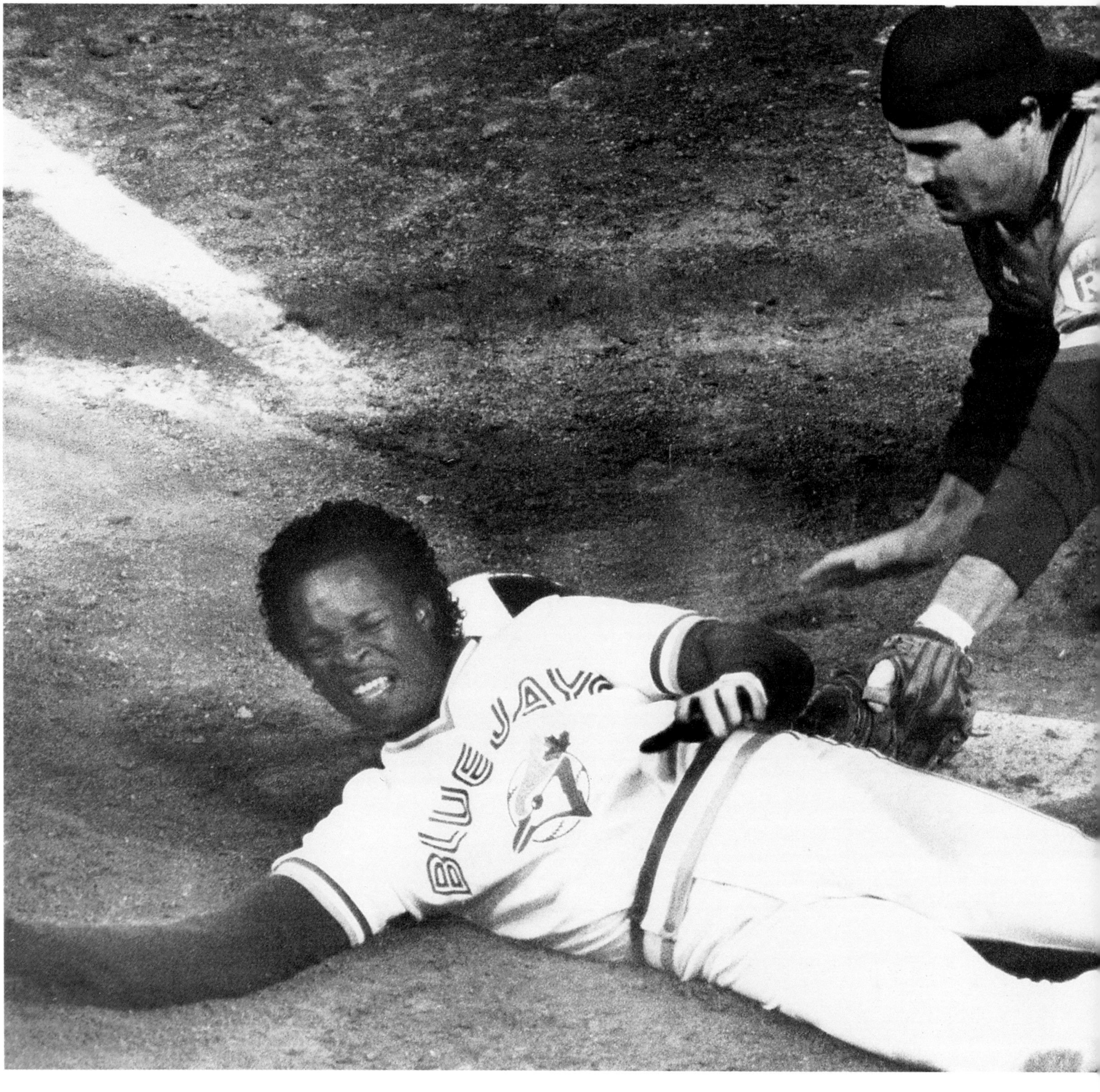

Above: *Tony Fernandez slides home with a tying run in the tenth inning of game two during the 1985 ALCS with the Kansas City Royals. The Blue Jays were to score again only moments later to grab a seemingly commanding 2-0 lead in the best-of-seven series.*

The Jays started fast enough in post-season play, clipping Kansas City in Toronto by scores of 6-1 and 6-5, the second game a 10-inning nail-biter with Henke relieving Key for the mound victory and Al Oliver singling home the winning run. After dropping a close 6-5 decision at Kansas City in game three, the Jays showed no signs of collapse, rebounding with a 3-1 victory in game four. And it was again Al Oliver who provided the fireworks, doubling home the game-winning runs with none out in the ninth. But the Jays seemed to run out of heroics at that point, and a pennant-clinching fourth victory proved all too elusive. Kansas City left-hander Danny Jackson shut down the Jays' bats in a 2-0 game five Royals win, and the Jays limped back to Canadian soil needing only a single home-field triumph to ice the pennant. But two key blows eventually did the Jays in – the first a third series homer by George Brett which put Kansas City out in front to stay in game six, and the second a crushing Jim Sundberg bases-loaded triple which broke open game seven. Dave Stieb – the victim of Sundberg's unlikely heroics – was later to comment that the sight of Sundberg's wind-blown fly bouncing atop the right-field fence was indeed the most painful memory

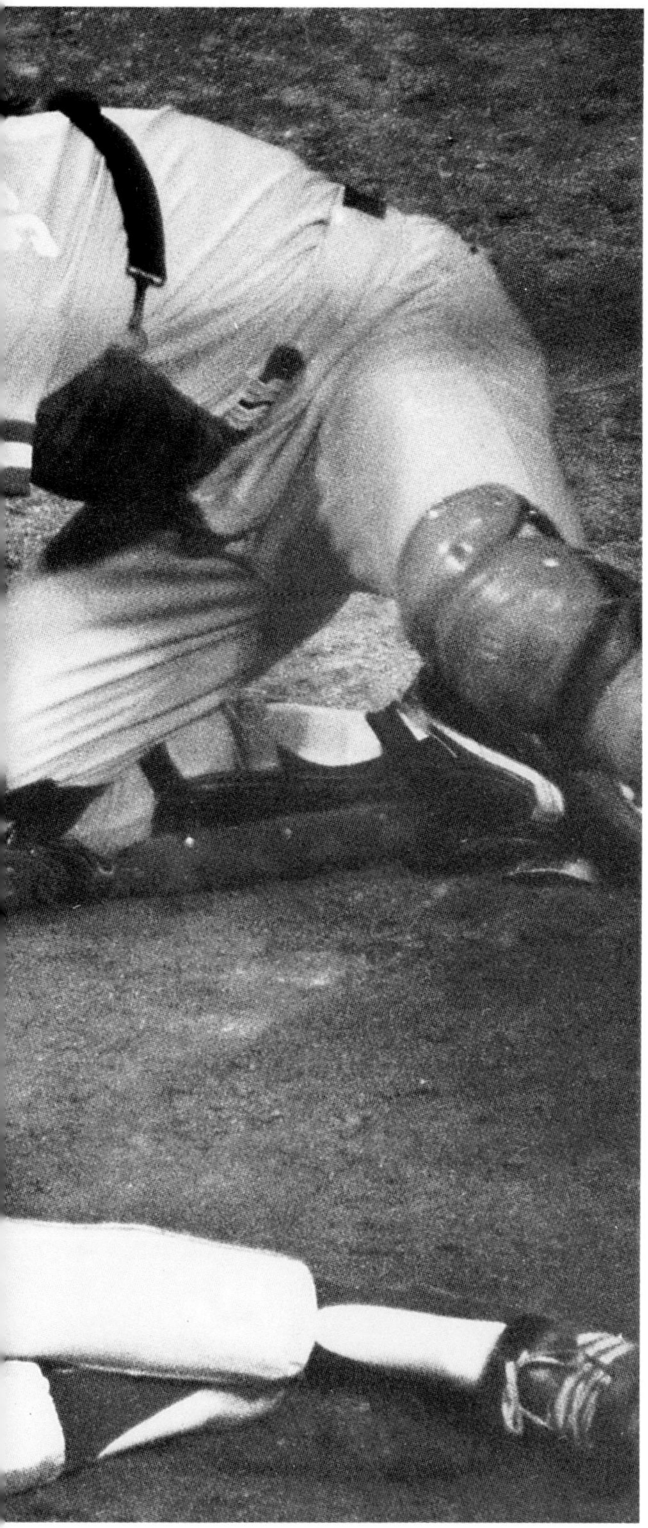

of his baseball career. And millions of Canadian fans could not have agreed more.

Disappointment over the loss to Kansas City was brief and stoically accepted by the resilient Toronto fans and young Blue Jay players. The Blue Jays had finally arrived at the top of the American League, after all, and there was always next year, when a World Championship now seemed all but certain. The Jays stood fast among the baseball elite, and Toronto fans were inclined to pay little heed to what had just happened before their very eyes during the summer of 1985 to those seemingly invincible Tigers, who had themselves reigned so supreme only a short summer earlier. But the Tigers of Detroit and the lessons of baseball's fickle fortunes would be back in all their glory in Exhibition Stadium before the next year of baseball had been played to its final out.

The most transparent reasons for the sudden on-field and off-field baseball successes enjoyed by Toronto's Blue Jays between expansion draft day in 1977 and the divisional title of 1985 are not hard to locate and explain. In his detailed study of the young Toronto franchise, sportswriter Larry Millson (*Ballpark Figures – The Blue Jays and the Business of Baseball*, 1987) carefully documents the role of Pat Gillick and his staff in constructing a minor league support system and major league front office staff with few parallels in baseball's long and storied management history. Gillick's contributions were also fittingly acknowledged by the baseball establishment at the end of the 1985 championship season when the veteran Toronto Vice-President for Baseball Operations was tabbed as organized baseball's major league Executive of the Year.

But perhaps the key, as Millson notes, is the degree to which the Blue Jays followed the sterling example of the Los Angeles Dodgers, and painstakingly developed continuity and franchise loyalty deep within Toronto's baseball organization. Former players were regularly hired back into the system as roving scouts, coaches and minor league managers (Doug Ault, John Mayberry, Bob Bailor, Hector Torres and Eddie Dennis are examples). Bob Mattick provided essential continuity throughout

Left: *Only days after the Blue Jays had been eliminated from ALCS play by the Royals, ex-Toronto manager Bobby Cox arrives to witness World Series play in St. Louis. Cox had just been named the new general manager of Atlanta's National League club, having been replaced by Jimy Williams as Blue Jays field boss.*

Above: *Nino Espinosa appeared in only one game for the Jays, his final big-league pitching appearance.*

Above right: *Epy Guerrero coordinates scouting and Latin American player development under the tutelage of Pat Gillick.*

Opposite: *This rare action shot captures a dramatic moment in Blue Jays history. Here Jays catcher Buck Martinez manages to make the tag on helpless Seattle Mariners runner Gorman Thomas, concluding a bizarre double play during which Martinez had already sprained his ankle while colliding at the plate with Seattle runner Phil Bradley.*

three phases of team development – as scouting supervisor (1977-1979), field manager (1980-1981), and Vice-President for Baseball Operations (1982-1988). The Latin American scouting and recruitment program under the astute management of Gillick and his hand-picked superscout Epy Guerrero has become a model unrivalled by previous major league baseball operations. By June 1985, Toronto employed 34 Latin Americans (23 Dominicans) throughout its major league and minor league systems, a pace-setting standard for either league; during spring training of 1989 the 16 Latin American players on the Blue Jays' 40-man roster was again the most in the majors by a wide margin (Pittsburgh was second with 11).

And yet for all the obvious successes there were also the inevitable storm clouds building along the horizon. World Championships and even Division Championships bring huge contract demands from star players, and winning teams are never as hungry on the field as losing teams, especially those victory-starved expansion teams. Millson underscores the paradox of the Blue Jays at the end of the 1985 season when he notes that owning a sports franchise confronts management with two distinct though not unrelated "bottom lines" as yardsticks to major league success. The fans are always aware of the first such measure – wins and losses, and championship flags joyously celebrated in the month of October. More subtle yet even more vital to franchise survival is the ledger-item of dollars and cents, and the unfortunate fact in Toronto is that it is always Canadian and not US dollars and cents that count.

By such a measure, the post-championship season was to become the team's worst year ever. In the face of the second largest attendance to date in Blue Jay history (2,455,477 paying customers) the organization still lost $3 million or perhaps more. The problem here, of course, was that $14 million (Canadian) in revenue had to sustain player payrolls and other burgeoning expenses to be paid out in US dollars, a losing proposition from the start. And 47,000-seat (standing-room capacity) Exhibition Stadium was already proving an unhealthy burden to the overtaxed Canadian-based franchise. While each sellout in Yankee Stadium meant $400,000-plus (US) to New York Yankees ownership, a sellout in Toronto would bring in only $250,000 (Canadian) to the Blue Jays' empty coffers. The long-awaited and hopefully more lucrative downtown SkyDome Stadium – scheduled to premier early in 1989 as perhaps baseball's finest facility – was now projected to be only several seasons away. But so was MVP slugger George Bell's $4.5 million, two-year contract!

5. There's No Easy Way to Get to "The Big Bird Feeder"

Below: *Reliable Rance Mulliniks at third base leaps to snag a line drive from the bat of Oriole Juan Bonilla in Exhibition Stadium action.*

Baseball tradition is forever inexorably bound up with the incomparable aura of historic baseball stadiums. The ballpark – site of memorable past triumphs as well as inglorious and heart-rending defeats – is the key element in each ball club's historical perception of itself. Modern-day players roam the same outfield grasses and circle the very same basepaths as legendary heroes of yesteryear; ancient ballparks link generations of old and new fans. Even baseball's most literate spokesman, author Roger Angell repeatedly articulates this preference, shared by most true fans, for teams instilled with rich baseball tradition – tradition fostered most effectively by legendary players and historic ballparks.

A novice ball club with little apparent claim on baseball history, Toronto's Blue Jays played out their first decade in one of baseball's most charming and unusual ballparks, a sporting arena which offered in special character what it lacked in decades of legendary event. While certainly not Fenway Park or Wrigley Field, Toronto's Exhibition Stadium earned in only a few short seasons a permanent place in both Canadian and American baseball lore and legend. No major league park has witnessed over the past decade a more lengthy litany of bizarre baseball moments. It was in "The X" alone that baseballs bounced wildly off the hidden concrete floor to float tauntingly over amazed infielders' heads; it was here that New York Yankee Dave Winfield struck down a helpless seagull with his infamous warm-up toss between innings; here that Lloyd Moseby once stole second and then first again in an unintentional re-enactment of an exploit by Detroit Tiger baseball clown Germany Schaefer of the Ty Cobb era; and here alone that each game ended with massive invasions of hungry seagulls befitting dark scenes from any of Hitchcock's most ominous cinematic thrillers.

Exhibition Stadium itself was often enough shortchanged by baseball fans who have not experienced its true charms first-hand. To rate this ballpark as the worst in the majors – as does author Bob Wood in his 1988 volume *Dodger Dogs to Fenway Franks - The Ultimate Guide to America's Top Baseball Parks* – is to judge baseball stadiums only in terms of creature comfort such as wind-chill factor and the plushness of contoured, padded seats. For author Wood, the Blue Jays' original home comes

in tied for last among major league parks, in a dead heat with the Houston Astrodome and just a whisker in unpleasantness ahead of Candlestick Park and the bland Seattle Kingdome. Ballpark fast-food, seating amenities, scoreboard aesthetics, ballpark employees, and stadium upkeep are among Wood's limited criteria for ranking North America's ballparks, and by these standards most of the quaint parks (Ebbets Field, Forbes Field, Sportsman's Park, and countless others) of an earlier age would also fail miserably. To complain that Exhibition Stadium was first and foremost "a plastic baseball diamond literally rolled on to a plastic football field" is to ignore the unavoidable fact that all newer major league facilities are by necessity multipurpose stadia, usually more suited to King Football than to the nation's summer pastime. Exhibition Stadium did have to its lasting credit – unlike prototypes in Cincinnati, Pittsburgh, St. Louis or San Diego – its traditionally rectangular baseball shape. And best of all, this often wintry ballpark managed to escape that most unpardonable breach of faith with fans that has marred other newly minted urban parks – it didn't remove fans hundreds of feet from the actual field of baseball play. This was a multipurpose stadium with a difference, of course, and there were compensating features as well. Absent was the oval shape of the typical football stadium, as well as the faint white football lines across outfield and infield surface often seen during

Above: *Jimmy Key is seen here en route to pitching the fifth one-hit game by a Toronto hurler, on May 22, 1986. Ozzie Guillen of the White Sox provided the lone blemish – a fifth-inning single – on Key's otherwise perfect night, a 5-0 victory at Chicago which snapped a seven-game winning streak for the host team.*

Above: *A wayward seagull finds itself in a somewhat tight spot here as Blue Jays outfielder Lloyd Moseby fields Willie Wilson's hit in the first inning of an August 1986 game with Kansas City. On this occasion the bird escaped but the ball didn't, as Moseby's adroit fielding held Wilson to a single on the play. Seagulls were a regular sight on the outfield turf of Exhibition Stadium, causing local patrons to refer regularly to the Toronto ballpark as "the Big Bird Feeder."*

August and September in other ballparks shared with NFL franchises. And the Monsanto baseball surface (at 160,000 square feet, the largest in North America) was a covering placed directly atop the football surface. The fact that most of the infield surface (including pitcher's mound, home plate, and first base) lay outside of the football playing area allowed as well for permanent installation of that part of the baseball surface.

Wood agrees that Exhibition Stadium had its plusses: "No major league ballpark enjoys a prettier setting. No other stroll from car to stadium is quite as inviting. Backed up against the bright blue waters of Lake Ontario, Exhibition Stadium . . . sits surrounded by the 300 acres of tidy green Exhibition Park. A few miles away a tight Toronto skyline says 'Hi.' Everything and everybody are pleasant." What more do we desire of our ballparks, especially the new and too-often multipurpose monoliths built primarily to serve NFL football?

While Exhibition Stadium admittedly boasted a somewhat strange appearance, with its covered left-field bleachers featuring contoured plastic seats, and its uncovered grandstands behind home plate and along the baselines befitting the aluminum benches of a college football stadium, this uniqueness was no less colorful than the architecture of such vaunted ancient parks as Braves Field in Boston, Sportsman's Park in St. Louis, or Crosley Field in Cincinnati. While overflow crowds at sellout games in Toronto throughout the mid-1980s would often leave some fans at a distant vantage point, several hundred feet beyond the right-field fence, the poorest seats were no worse than the obstructed-view locations often sold at the older-style ballyards such as Comiskey Park or Tiger Stadium. The distant right-field locations of Exhibition Stadium were, in fact, no further from home plate than the deep center-field bleachers in one of baseball's most ballyhooed arenas – the ancient Polo Grounds in Harlem, which served the New York Giants so proudly for decades and which featured a shape and construction far from consistent with the average fan's notion of what an ideal ballpark should be. Among the newer parks, Exhibition Stadium was in fact distinctive in its unique shape and its total freedom from the "oval sameness" of other multipurpose stadia; and box seat locations along the baselines provided Toronto fans with an intimate on-field closeness matched only by tiny spring training facilities of Florida or Arizona.

Yet it was always the special character of Exhibition Stadium – nestled between ferris wheels and carnival booths within the Canadian National Exhibition grounds – which lent the Jays' home ballpark its special charm. No out-of-town visitor attending Blue Jay games soon forgot the ever-circling flocks of St. Lawrence seagulls which descended upon the popcorn-rich bleachers as fans departed during late innings of one-sided games. The "Big Bird Feeder" has also been affectionately labelled by more than one Toronto baseball writer as Canada's single contribution to American baseball humor. And the reputation seems duly earned. High bounces off the concrete-like artificial playing surface often caused outfielders to wait in frustration for careening baseballs to return to earth as runners gleefully circled the base-paths.

One result of the rock-like playing surface at "The X" was that games sometimes appeared to be contested with a maple stick and a tennis ball rather than with ash bat and horsehide hardball. It is in this park as well that Lloyd Moseby stole second, returned to first (after failing to pick up the location of an errantly thrown ball from White Sox catcher Carlton Fisk), and then stole second yet another time on the same

play during a July 1987 game. And it is in this same park that Yankee outfielder Dave Winfield once kayoed a low swooping seagull with a thrown ball during inter-inning outfield warmups in 1983, a happenstance that today looms as baseball's most infamous deadtime incident. And Exhibition Stadium will live on in the memory of every American League fan for its opening game of 1977, the only major league game ever played throughout its entirety in a relentless subarctic blizzard.

Some of the most lofty moments of Blue Jay history are also interwoven with the special ambience of now moribund Exhibition Stadium. This ballpark has been home not only to some of the most fabled moments of Toronto sports history, but also to several of baseball's most unforgettable events of the past decade. First there was Toronto's 9-0 forfeit victory over the Baltimore Orioles on September 15, 1977, a game in which starter Jim Clancy had held the Birds scoreless on two hits over five innings before Manager Earl Weaver pulled his Oriole team off the playing field in vehement protest. Weaver's later unsuccessful contention was that the bullpen tarps constituted an unacceptable playing hazard for his infielders in the chasing of foul balls.

Above: *Workmen clear snow from the center-field bleacher seats at Exhibition Stadium on March 30, 1987 – just seven days prior to a Blue Jays' scheduled home opener versus the Cleveland Indians.*

Left: *Jim Clancy remains the only Blue Jays pitcher other than Dave Stieb to win more than 100 games in the Toronto uniform.*

Rising to the height of a 31-story building, the retractable roof of the new SkyDome Stadium looms over the exterior of the in-stadium hotel. The resulting spectacle is hardly the expected exterior face of a traditional major league ballpark, and Toronto's SkyDome is anything but traditional. Built at a cost of more than $400 million and costing in excess of 10,000 person-years of employment, this futuristic park assures that in Toronto the old saying "take me out to the ballgame" will never be quite the same.

On June 26, 1978 – again versus Baltimore and Earl Weaver – the Jays erupted for an impressive 24-10 victory, the team's highest scoring game ever and one of the highest in major league history. The Baltimore Orioles, in fact, seemingly took special delight in playing doormat to the Blue Jays in Exhibition Stadium. Thus it was Baltimore who was again victimized on September 14, 1987 by an unprecedented Toronto offensive uprising. In this latter game the Jays exploded for a major league record 10 home runs while pounding out an 18-3 drubbing of hapless Baltimore. On that memorable afternoon Ernie Whitt (3), George Bell (2), Rance Mulliniks (2), Fred McGriff, Rob Ducey, and Lloyd Moseby all contributed to the record-setting onslaught of Toronto round-trippers. A second major league standard reached on this same memorable afternoon was a record for most players on one team simultaneously enjoying multiple-home-run games. Yet another and perhaps more unusual "first" in this September 1987 slugfest was that Baltimore manager Cal Ripken Sr. seized the hopeless situation to replace his son, Cal Ripken Jr., at shortstop during the eighth inning, bringing to an end iron-man Ripken's unprecedented streak of 8243 consecutive innings played. "What the hell," quipped the senior Ripken in reference to the one-sided score and his son's consecutive-inning streak, "he couldn't have hit a 20-run homer!"

When Exhibition Stadium hosted its final game early in its thirteenth season, it had already left a legacy that some parks achieve only after decades of major league play.

But all the baseball joys and frustrations of Exhibition Stadium were to come to a premature end in early June of 1989. And the final game in "The X" – played at the end of the final May homestand – was a fitting enough swan song for a stadium already so rich in local baseball lore. Again the opponent was the Chicago White Sox, ironically and perhaps not accidentally the very same club that had helped the expansion Blue Jays christen "The X" 13 years earlier. And a Hollywood scriptwriter could not have provided a better ending. The teams battled into extra innings before a standing-room-only Sunday crowd drenched with a party atmosphere and waiting to explode one final time at the least excuse of home team heroics. With the score at 5-5 in the bottom of the tenth, Toronto's one true legitimate superstar of the first decade, George Bell, crushed a Bobby Thigpen fastball high into the famous left-field bleachers for a fitting two-run game-ending homer. To the other bizarre legacies of Toronto's Exhibition Stadium could now be added yet another singular distinction. Exhibition Stadium was the only major league park whose last big-league pitch had dramatically resulted in a game-winning homer.

Toronto's baseball establishment had remained sensitive from the beginning to the inefficiencies and inconveniences of playing baseball in a temporary makeshift park designed primarily for the rival autumn game of football. The long-planned replacement for Exhibition Stadium, officially launched with formal ground-breaking ceremonies in October 1986, was from the first envisioned by club officials as an ultimate showcase for contemporary baseball – the diamond sport's first multipurpose stadium with retractable dome roof, a true futuristic facility providing all the conveniences and luxuries of an indoor arena and yet allowing for outdoor baseball as well on sunbaked summer days. Unique features of Toronto's unprecedented new SkyDome baseball home would include a retractable roof capable of opening or closing in as little as 20 minutes; 100 percent uncovered playing surface (with 91 percent uncovered seats) featured under open-air playing conditions; and even a 364-suite hotel complex at the north-end of the stadium featuring approximately 70 rooms overlooking the actual field of play. Located at the foot of the landmark CN Tower in the heart of downtown Toronto, baseball's newest architectural wonder holds out promise as the most revolutionary ballpark in major league

Left: *Huge gargoyle caricatures of baseball fans drape from the exterior facade of the new SkyDome Stadium, providing a humorous and eyecatching welcome for visitors to Toronto's new plush downtown ballpark.*

Below: *Kelly Gruber awaits a pitch during the second week of SkyDome action versus the Seattle Mariners. Scott Bradley is the Seattle catcher.*

Above: *Preparations continue inside the SkyDome as participants in the opening night ceremonies run through a final mid-week rehearsal for the spectacular dedication gala event. As this May 31st scene took place, city officials had still not been granted final clearance from safety inspectors to open the huge stadium on time for its scheduled June 3rd premier event.*

Opposite: *Fireworks explode within and over Toronto's new landmark wonder – the SkyDome Stadium – as the grand finale of dedication night ceremonies draws to its colorful conclusion. This gala affair was held two nights before the first major league game was played in baseball's most modern and luxurious facility.*

history – a true twenty-first-century edifice designed to luxuriously accommodate America's indigenous nineteenth-century game. The impact of this futuristic stadium upon the game of baseball it houses promises to be the most radical yet witnessed in this modern age of multipurpose stadia. The possibility of closing or opening the stadium roof in such short time periods has already prompted the American League rules committee to consider new standards to cover special circumstances of rain delays arising during play in the Toronto SkyDome.

As the 1989 season opened in wintry Toronto in April, the SkyDome was still two months away from becoming a baseball reality – delayed by numerous construction setbacks, plagued by astronomical cost overruns, site of continuing labor difficulties, and recipient of bad press of every imaginable sort. Major controversies had continuously arisen concerning anticipated parking inadequacies and huge projected transportation gridlocks to be encountered daily when Toronto fans began flocking to the downtown stadium by the middle of the 1989 season. But whatever the political issues and public alarm surrounding construction of baseball's first moveable-roof stadium, the Toronto SkyDome was finally on schedule to become a reality by early June of 1989, and with it an era would end and another would begin. Indoor baseball – at least partially indoor baseball – would at last come to the one city where perhaps the often frigid weather actually justifies such an anomaly. And civic pride had already been buoyed in late 1988 with announcements that the Queen City of Toronto – still awaiting its first World Series – would reap the honor of hosting its first Major League All-Star Game during the upcoming 1990 season.

Perhaps the most remembered Toronto baseball night for years to come will be the inaugural SkyDome game played on Monday, June 5, 1989, against the Milwaukee Brewers. A franchise record crowd of 48,378 witnessed the first pitch thrown by Jimmy Key to Milwaukee leadoff hitter Paul Molitor. The first at-bat in the new stadium also resulted in the first hit, as Molitor slammed Key's third delivery past diving shortstop Tony Fernandez into the left-field gap for a game-opening double. The first home run was appropriately slugged by Fred McGriff in the second inning, a game-tying two-run blast off Brewer right-hander Don August. George Bell was to homer later that night as well, as he had done in the final game at Exhibition Stadium, but this time the outcome was to be different and the slumping Jays lost out to the Brewers by the count of 5-3. But in the end the record Toronto crowd went home thrilled with the new ballpark, one that even baseball purists had to admit was a marvel of technology and a wonder of baseball-viewing luxury.

The Jays started surprisingly slow in their new home, not able to break the doldrums that had been plaguing them all season. On August 1, after two months of SkyDome play, the Blue Jays were still a game under .500 and trailing the seemingly unflappable Orioles. But by the last month of the season, with improved pitching and a rejuvenated offense inspired by George Bell and newcomer Mookie Wilson, Toronto was suddenly nearly unbeatable at home and the stage was set to close out the season with two of the most important and thrilling games in Blue Jay history. Fittingly the opposition would be the familiar Orioles, who led the league for most of the season, but also the very team that had played so many memorable games in Toronto in little over a decade of American League Eastern Division rivalry. The young Baltimore team came to Toronto for the last weekend of the season needing a series sweep to wrest the pennant from the front-running Jays, and as was fitting, the new stadium itself was destined to play a role in the subsequent pennant-race drama. The cavernous SkyDome surroundings led to two low-scoring defensive games, as had been the case in most play since opening night four months earlier. And a piece of irony came into play as well on Friday, September 29, as construction debris surrounding the unfinished ballpark would also provide a bizarre, final blow to the Orioles' pennant dream.

WORKS, TORONTO!

Below: *Despite his poor year at the plate in 1989, Lloyd Moseby proved the batting hero when the chips were down, knocking home the extra-inning run that clinched a division flag.*

Below right: *George Bell provided the final fireworks in the title-clincher with a game-winning sacrifice fly which preserved the 4-3 hard-earned victory.*

The opening game of the crucial season-ending series was a nail-biter down to the very end. Veteran Lloyd Moseby emerged as the eventual batting hero on what proved for 10 gripping innings to be largely a pitcher's night. Redeeming himself from a poor offensive season (.221 BA with only 43 RBIs), Moseby sliced a drive off the left-field fence in the bottom of the eleventh to ice a hard-earned 2-1 Toronto victory. The Jays had trailed 1-0 (Phil Bradley of Baltimore opened the game with a homer on the night's first pitch) before reliever Gregg Olson had wild-pitched home the tying run in the bottom of the eighth. But the most dramatic development took place an hour or more after the game's conclusion. Pete Harnish, scheduled to start game two for Baltimore, was injured walking to his hotel room when he stepped on a rusty nail in the construction-littered walkways just outside the SkyDome. With Harnish unable to make his start on Saturday, substitute rookie Dave Johnson pitched brilliantly enough in his stead, taking a 3-1 lead into the eighth inning before succumbing to eventual wildness. For the second straight day Baltimore reliever Mark Williamson was victimized by a last-ditch Toronto rally as Liriano singled home two runs and George Bell pounded out the game-winning sacrifice fly that preserved a 4-3 victory and set off a massive but orderly celebration throughout the joyous city of Toronto and across the proud nation of Canada. At slightly after 3:30P.M. on September 30 the Skydome witnessed its first championship celebration, only 53 games and a little under four months into its brief but already lively baseball history.

From its opening night Toronto's new SkyDome has been a marketing success, if not entirely a baseball one. Players (especially those of visiting teams) early on complained about the swirling winds that whipped through the uncovered dome and seemed to make the SkyDome an American League equivalent of San Francisco's notorious Candlestick Park. Fans as well are distracted from the game itself by the mere spectacle of the nine-story-high center-field scoreboard (built by Sony and measuring 35-by-115 feet) and its high-resolution, Diamond-Vision picture. All the bugs hadn't yet been removed from the stadium when it opened and the third game in the opening series against Milwaukee was ironically delayed by rain for almost two

hours when the not yet fully automatic roof would not shut properly. But despite these inevitable glitches, fans poured into the new dome at record numbers, exceeding 49,000 a game. By season's end, aided by 53 home dates in the popular dome, the Jays had reached a new American League attendance mark of 3,375,573, far outstripping the existing mark set only a season earlier in Minnesota by the defending World Champion Twins. A first-time-ever season of four million-plus home patrons is even a reasonable goal, with an average-game attendance of more than 45,000 a proper expectation. The Skydome of Toronto – like Walter O'Malley's Dodgers Stadium three decades earlier – has already become baseball's new unchallenged showcase arena.

Above: *A panoramic right-field view of SkyDome action between the Blue Jays and Oakland Athletics in mid-July, a preview of the 1989 ALCS to follow in October.*

6. "El Beisbol" North of the Border

From the honor roll of brilliant shortstops in the 1950s (Chico Carrasquel, Luis Aparicio, Leo Cardenas, Willie Miranda, Chico Fernandez, Jose Valdivielso, Ruben Amaro, Jose Pagan, Zoilo Versalles) to the strong-armed hurlers (Juan Marichal, Mike Cuellar, Luis Tiant) and adept batsmen (Roberto Clemente, Orlando Cepeda, Minnie Minoso, Rico Carty) of the 1960s, on to the current crop of Spanish-speaking superstars (Canseco, Valenzuela, and the Blue Jays' own George Bell), the Latin American impact on the majors has been inescapable in recent decades. During the 1980s, especially, the flow of baseball talent from "south of the border" has reached near floodtide proportions, and would be far greater yet if not for U.S. immigration policies limiting current foreign-born players in organized baseball to a maximum number of 500.

Baseball is ultimately a game of statistics, of course, and with Latin immigration the numbers speak loudly for themselves. *Baseball America*'s 1985 survey of major league farm systems revealed that 349 professional players under contract to major league teams (as of June 1985) claimed Latin American birthright. Among that number the tally was as follows: 163 Dominicans, 93 Puerto Ricans, 52 Venezuelans, 18 Mexicans, 10 Panamanians, 9 Cubans, 3 Colombians, and a single Nicaraguan. And it was the Blue Jays with 34 Latin Americans (23 Dominicans) who not surprisingly led all big-league clubs in

Below: *Luis Leal delivers a pitch in Exhibition Stadium, with Latin teammate Tony Fernandez poised at shortstop. Leal was one of the first members of Toronto's famed Latin American baseball connection.*

Latin American recruitment, followed at some distance by the Pittsburgh Pirates with 25 (18 Dominicans). The "Dominican connection" (highlighted by George Bell's 1987 American League MVP season) has long been the centerpiece and showcase of this Latin baseball talent pool. The mid-sized island city of San Pedro de Macoris – as most informed baseball fans know – has achieved a certain measure of fame as a remarkable fountainhead of major league talent. With a population of a little over 125,000, San Pedro itself has supplied over 270 talented prospects to organized baseball in the past two decades, and 15 big leaguers presently hail from this single Dominican baseball hot spot. In this number we can include the following: Joaquin Andujar, Pedro Guerrero, ex-Blue Jay shortstop Alfredo Griffin, Julio Franco, former Blue Jay slugger Rico Carty, and of course George Bell and Tony Fernandez.

When the boys of summer launched their Grapefruit League and Cactus League seasons this past spring, a total of 156 Latin players (14.8 percent of the total 1040) stocked the 40-man rosters of the 26 big-league clubs. These numbers broke down further into 96 American Leaguers (16.8 percent of the league's total players) and 60 National Leaguers (12.5 percent), and it was again Toronto boasting the largest current number (14) of Hispanic players. The current crop of Latin American major leaguers in 1989's spring camps included 53 pitchers, 13 catchers, 58 infielders, and 32 flycatchers.

No team has exploited this new Caribbean basin baseball talent pool as efficiently and with as much foresight as have the Toronto Blue Jays under the leadership of GM Pat Gillick and his hand-picked Latin American scouting coordinator, Epy Guerrero. Gillick's reliance on Latin American scouting reflects a long-standing policy of the Blue Jays' organization to build quickly by circumventing the normal amateur draft of US college and high school playing talent. The normal draft procedure has largely proven a disappointment for the Toronto franchise, providing only Lloyd Moseby (number one pick in 1978) through the conventional channels of player procurement. Gillick has turned instead to a long-standing working arrangement with Guerrero, a skillful talent sleuth who works out of Santo Domingo in the Dominican Republic and who was an early associate during Gillick's own earlier player development assignments with the Houston Astros and New York Yankees. The marriage had been a most successful one as the Jays have held regular clinics, built training facilities, and taken other concrete steps to maintain high visibility and increasing popularity among the baseball-crazed Dominican youth. And of course the unmatched popularity of the Jays in the Dominican Republic has received its greatest boost from the on-field successes in recent years of such heroic native sons as Alfredo Griffin, Tony Fernandez and the lionized George Bell.

A Dominican youngster receives pitching pointers from Epy Guerrero during a Blue Jays instructional camp in the island nation which is today's hotbed of baseball talent. Through the end of the 1988 season, approximately 475 Latin ballplayers had made it to the big leagues – with more than 70 percent of these having appeared since the relaxation of baseball's noxious color barriers at the end of World War II.

If the Blue Jays, under the administration of Gillick, have fostered the largest recent pool of Latin players, it was the Washington Senators of the late 1940s and early 1950s who first exploited the rich vein of Caribbean and South American baseball talent. Scout Joe Cambria unlocked the Cuban connection for Clark Griffith's lowly Senators in the immediate post-war period, and at a time when the Senators maintained only six farm clubs and three full-time scouts (by far the lowest in the majors), and chose to scout seriously only along the eastern seaboard region and throughout the Caribbean. While Griffith's penny-pinching plan for garnering cheap talent won few ball games for the hapless Nats of the 1950s, the influx of superb Latin players like Camilo Pascual, Pedro Ramos, Jose Valdivielso, Julio Becquer, Carlos Paula, Sandy Consuegra, Mike Fornieles, and dozens more, not only salvaged the ailing Washington franchise but also opened the eyes of competing GMs to the seemingly rich and untapped pool of Latin American player talent.

Right: *Mexican standout Jorge Orta served with four AL clubs and one NL team, compiling 1619 hits in a career that stretched over 16 seasons. Orta served one season (1983) as the inconsistent yet colorful Toronto DH.*

Far right: *Luis Gomez recorded 21 sacrifice hits and stalwart defensive play during two brief seasons at the end of the 1970s with the Blue Jays.*

Latin American immigration into the big leagues did not, of course, begin with the Senators in the 1950s any more than it began with the Blue Jays and Pat Gillick in the 1980s. The first recorded Latin American big leaguer played, in actuality, during the very infancy of the professional game we know today. His name was Esteban Enrique Bellan – a man later recognized as the "Father of Cuban Baseball" – and he patrolled several infield positions for the National Association's Troy Haymakers and New York Mutuals between 1871 and 1873. An early-day Latin star of the more modern era was another Cuban sensation, Adolfo "Dolf" Luque, a strong-armed right-hander who amassed 193 big-league victories while hurling for the Cincinnati Reds, Brooklyn Dodgers and New York Giants between 1914 and 1935. Luque, one of the more dominant pitchers of his day, once registered 27 victories in a single campaign (1923) and led the National League twice in ERA.

But most Latin American baseball players in the era of Bellan and the period of Dolph Luque were dark of skin and negroid of features and thus had no more opportunity than North American-born black athletes to display their talents in big-league ballparks across the land. Many of the Caribbean's greatest ballplayers of the decades between the two world wars – multi-talented ballplayers like Cuban Hall of Famer Martin Dihigo (the only man ever to be elected to three national baseball halls of fame) or strapping Cuban outfielder Cristobal Torriente – were left no alternative but to seek their limited baseball reputations in the Negro Leagues and Mexican League, or to toil periodically in winter league play against barnstorming teams comprised of their lighter-skinned big-league counterparts.

Yet once opportunities were open to Latin players, many big-league teams have greatly benefited from their skilled play and spirited presence. Among the first teams to exploit a burgeoning Latin American talent pool were the Pittsburgh Pirates (whose showcase player was the greatest Latin batsman of all time, Roberto Clemente) and the Brooklyn (later Los Angeles) Dodgers (who originally signed Clemente as a bonus baby but then lost him to a free-agent draft). But the recent edge indisputably goes to the Blue Jays, in raw talent as well as in mere numbers. Below are brief profiles of a dozen Latin American-born players who have impacted most greatly on Blue Jay baseball fortunes over the past decade or slightly more.

Jorge Orta (B. Mazatlan, Mexico, November 26, 1950). Jorge Orta made only a brief one-year stopover in Toronto during a distinguished 16-year big-league career. Yet his contribution was not insignificant during the Jays' first plus-.500 season, as the spray-hitting, part-time outfielder combined with another new acquisition – Cliff Johnson – to lift the Toronto DH position from one of the worst to one of the best in the American League. Obtained from the Mets in February of 1983 for minor league hurler Steve Senteney, Orta hit .237 in 103 games for Toronto, with 10 homers and 38 RBIs. Later that same winter he was traded away again, to Kansas City, for erratic hitter Willie Mays Aikens.

Jorge Orta's Major League Totals
Chicago (A) (1972-1979), Cleveland (1980-1981), Los Angeles (1982), Toronto (1983), Kansas City (1985-1987)

BA	G	AB	R	H	2B	3B	HR	RBI
.278	1755	5829	733	1619	267	63	130	745

Luis Gomez (B. Guadalajara, Mexico, August 19, 1951). Luis Gomez was the regular Toronto shortstop in 1978, batting .223 and contributing steady if not spectacular infield play. Gomez holds a trivial niche in Blue Jay history, however, as he lays claim to being the ball club's first free-agent signee. In the 1979 season Gomez split time at three infield positions in only 59 game appearances, as rookie sensation Alfredo Griffin had taken full command of the shortstop duties for the Jays' third season of play. Luis Gomez was subsequently expendable, and he was traded away to the Atlanta Braves in December of 1979 (along with Chris Chambliss, who never actually played a game in a Toronto uniform) for outfielder Barry Bonnell and pitcher Joey McLaughlin.

Luis Gomez's Major League Totals
Minnesota (1974-1977), Toronto (1978-1979), Atlanta (1980-1981)

BA	G	AB	R	H	2B	3B	HR	RBI
.210	609	1251	108	263	26	5	0	90

Damaso Garcia (B. Moca, Dominican Republic, February 7, 1957). Arriving from the Yankees in November 1979, in a major deal that also hailed the arrival of Chris Chambliss (soon dealt to Atlanta) and pitcher Paul Mirabella, and marked the departure of hurler Tom Underwood and catcher Rick Cerone, Dominican infielder Damaso Garcia immediately became a fixture at second base in Exhibition Stadium with a solid .278 BA and outstanding defensive play. Serving seven full seasons in Toronto before injuries hastened his departure in 1986, Garcia is the obvious choice as the best second sacker in Blue Jay history. At this date Garcia (recently a comeback player with the Montreal Expos) still holds Toronto single-season club records for stolen bases (54 in 1982), hitting streak (21 games in 1983), and being hit by pitched balls (9 times in 1984).

Damaso Garcia's Major League Totals
New York (A) (1978-1979), Toronto (1980-1986)

BA	G	AB	R	H	2B	3B	HR	RBI
.286	931	3651	461	1046	173	26	32	301

Above: *Surehanded Dominican infielder Damaso Garcia might well have been the Toronto second baseman for years to come had it not been for nagging injuries and the improved play of his younger countrymen, Nelson Liriano and Manny Lee.*

Left: *Dominican shortstop Alfredo Griffin was AL Rookie of the Year in 1979, but again a wealth of Latin American talent at the middle infield positions – this time Tony Fernandez – soon made the speedy Griffin expendable.*

Alfredo Griffin (B. Santo Domingo, Dominican Republic, March 6, 1957). Before Tony Fernandez, Alfredo Griffin was the ranking

Dominican Manny Lee is something of a rarity in the ranks of Toronto's Latin American players, having completed one year of college in his native land before signing a big-league contract. Lee was originally signed by the Mets, and was drafted by the Blue Jays out of the Houston Astros' organization.

shortstop of the Blue Jays' brief franchise history, and his 1979 rookie campaign (in which he shared freshman-of-the-year honors with John Castino of Minnesota) is still one of the finest ever enjoyed by a Toronto infielder. The emergence of his countryman Fernandez made Griffin expendable by the conclusion of the 1984 campaign, but not before the talented Dominican infielder (now playing with the Los Angeles Dodgers) established career team marks for sacrifice hits (67) and triples (50, since surpassed by Lloyd Moseby), and the single-season record for triples (15 in 1980) as well.

Alfredo Griffin's Major League Totals
Cleveland (1976-1978), Toronto (1979-1984), Oakland (1985-1987), Los Angeles (1988)

BA	G	AB	R	H	2B	3B	HR	RBI
.256	1466	5218	609	1326	191	71	23	423

Juan Beniquez (B. San Sebastian, Puerto Rico, May 13, 1950). Acquired from the Kansas City Royals for pitcher Luis Aquino on July 14, 1987, Beniquez was a major force in the Jays' ill-fated pennant drive late in the 1987 season. Hitting a solid .284 in the DH role, the Puerto Rican veteran of 16 previous big-league seasons and seven previous ball clubs provided several clutch game-winning hits in the waning days of August and September. Injuries slowed the veteran in 1988 and while he hit an improved .293 from the DH slot in his final Blue Jay season, Beniquez saw action in only 30 games in the summer of 1988.

Juan Beniquez's Blue Jay Totals
Toronto (1987-1988)

BA	G	AB	R	H	2B	3B	HR	RBI
.288	69	139	15	40	5	1	6	29

Manny Lee (B. San Pedro de Macoris, Dominican Republic, June 17, 1965). Manny Lee's one moment of big-league pressure has so far been the final week of the disastrous 1987 pennant stand when the inexperienced second-year infielder (veteran of only 80-plus ball games at the time) was called upon to fill in for injured shortstop Tony Fernandez in the final two crucial series with the pennant-winning Tigers. Over this stretch Lee hit .226 (7 for 31) and played an admirable defensive shortstop, marred only by a crucial misplayed ball which contributed to defeat in the season's penultimate game. By 1988, however, Manny Lee was seeing more regular duty, starting 94 games at second base and hitting an admirable .291 for the campaign.

Manny Lee's Blue Jay Totals
Toronto (1986-1989)

BA	G	AB	R	H	2B	3B	HR	RBI
.265	370	920	96	244	27	9	7	90

Alexis Infante (B. Barquisimeto, Venezuela, December 4, 1961). Enjoying banner seasons at Triple-A Syracuse in 1987 and 1988, Alexis Infante might already be a major league shortstop for any organization not already blessed with the talents of Tony Fernandez and well fortified with quality utility infielders like Manny Lee, Nelson Liriano and Tom Lawless. Following in the footsteps of his countrymen Luis Leal and Fred Manrique, Infante is the third Venezuelan native to play for the Jays and may well be the most talented player in the Toronto minor league system. It remains to be seen, however, whether blinding speed on the basepaths and a .300-plus Triple-A BA will be enough to dislodge the superb glove work of Fernandez, Liriano or Manny Lee.

Alexis Infante's Minor League Totals
Syracuse (1984-1988)

BA	G	AB	R	H	2B	3B	HR	RBI
.247	469	1530	205	386	44	16	6	119

Sil Campusano (B. Mano Guayabo, Dominican Republic, December 31, 1966). The 1989 season was the second summer during which Sil Campusano was expected to crack the Jays' starting outfield, dislodging veterans like Moseby, Barfield or Bell. It was also the second consecutive year in which the young and diminutive Dominican outfielder quickly played himself off the roster, earning a quick trip back to Syracuse in the International League with his inability to hit a major league breaking ball. Campusano has the defensive skills if not the bat to see big-league service, but with the increasing talent pool of young outfielders in Toronto (Rob Ducey, Junior Felix, Glenn Allen Hill and Kevin Batiste) time may be growing short for this once highly touted prospect.

Sil Campusano's Blue Jay Totals
Toronto (1988)

BA	G	AB	R	H	2B	3B	HR	RBI
.218	73	142	14	31	10	2	2	12

Nelson Liriano (B. Puerto Plata, Dominican Republic, June 3, 1964). A solid defensive replacement and pesky hitter, Nelson Liriano will perhaps best be remembered in subsequent years as the utility player who twice in the early season of 1989 broke up no-hit games (one by Kirk McCaskill of the Angels and the other by Nolan Ryan of the Rangers) with two outs in the final inning of play. Liriano showed steady improvement at the plate in 1989, batting .263 and knocking home 53 runs in part-time play, and this speedy Dominican role player may yet emerge as the sure-handed Toronto second baseman of the future.

Nelson Liriano's Blue Jay Totals
Toronto (1987-1989)

BA	G	AB	R	H	2B	3B	HR	RBI
.259	268	853	116	221	38	7	10	86

Junior Felix (B. Laguna Sabada, Dominican Republic, October 3, 1967). Junior Felix was one of the major surprises of the 1989 season, a solid contributor in right field throughout much of the summer and a serious Rookie of the Year candidate until an early August shoulder separation from which the Dominican youngster never fully recovered over the final two months of the campaign. Blessed with blazing speed, the switch-hitting Felix was originally discovered by superscout Epy Guerrero while competing in a Dominican track meet – Felix had almost no formal baseball ex-

Below: *Signed by Blue Jays superscout Epy Guerrero, Dominican second baseman Nelson Liriano began his professional career in 1982 and had advanced to the major league roster only four seasons later. The everyday second baseman in 1988, Liriano accepted a utility roll in 1989 and earned notoriety by breaking up two no-hitters with his ninth-inning clutch base hits.*

Above: *George Bell emerged from a stormy 1988 season to spark the Blue Jays down the stretch in 1989 and establish himself as a serious league MVP candidate. Bell is today the ranking national hero in a Dominican Republic nation known for its seemingly endless crop of fine major league stars.*

perience until a scant three years ago. Junior arrived in Toronto with a bang on May 4th, slugging a homer on his first major league pitch against the California Angels, thus becoming only the eleventh player in big-league history to achieve such a feat. It was, in fact, Felix's power display that surprised the Blue Jays' brain trust in 1989, as the diminutive outfielder connected for nine homers, three times his minor league total for the previous season.

Junior Felix's Minor League Totals
Knoxville, Southern Association (1988)

BA	G	AB	R	H	2B	3B	HR	RBI
.253	93	360	52	91	16	5	3	25

George Bell (B. San Pedro de Macoris, Dominican Republic, October 21, 1959). George Bell's banner American League seasons of 1987 and 1989 have brought him the status of national hero in the Dominican Republic and earned personal wealth which boggles the mind by the standards of his poor island homeland. Yet Bell's popularity in North America's big-league cities has not approached his adoration throughout Latin America, and the Blue Jays' enigmatic MVP slugger remains a player reviled by fans and press alike for his sullen personality and outspoken, quick-triggered reactions to the pressures of major league celebrity status. Bell's bat did most of his talking over the second half of the recent American League campaign, however, turning hometown jeers to cheers as he personally carried the Jays' often inconsistent offense down the stretch to their second divisional title in 1989. A subject of constant trade rumors and admittedly a defensive liability with his shaky left-field play, Bell remains at the close of the 1989 season the one true superstar of the first epoch of Toronto Blue Jay history.

George Bell's Blue Jay Totals
Toronto (1981-1989)

BA	G	AB	R	H	2B	3B	HR	RBI
.289	1039	3966	574	1145	212	32	182	654

Tony Fernandez (B. San Pedro de Macoris, Dominican Republic, June 30, 1962). Committing only six errors over the full season, Tony Fernandez established a new major league standard in 1989 for defensive brilliance at the shortstop position, a position he has dominated in American League play for much of the past several seasons. Many veteran observers argue that Fernandez is indeed the best defensive shortstop in baseball today, if not the best ever, and his offensive skills clearly vault him into that position ahead of such other defensive wizards as Ozzie Smith of the Cardinals and Alfredo Griffin of the Dodgers. You certainly would find little argument in Canada that Tony Fernandez has been the very heart and soul of the Blue Jay franchise over the past several seasons, and it was a key injury to their brilliant shortstop that played a far greater role in the Jays' 1987 pennant collapse than did the untimely team batting slump or hitting failures of George Bell over the team's final seven games.

Tony Fernandez's Blue Jay Totals
Toronto (1983-1989)

BA	G	AB	R	H	2B	3B	HR	RBI
.292	867	3317	426	967	165	44	36	338

As Toronto sportswriter Larry Millson has aptly observed, remove the Latin American influence (more specifically the Dominican Republic factor) from the story of the Toronto Blue Jays and you remove the heart of a team that has compiled the best overall record in baseball since 1985. Much of the Blue Jays' early success in the mid-1980s can be attributed directly to the stellar defensive play by the doubleplay combination of Tony Fernandez and Damaso Garcia, and Nelson Liriano and Manny Lee have admirably taken up the slack at second base left by Garcia's departure. George Bell's booming bat and MVP years carried the Jays through the stretch run of both division title seasons. With the arrival of Junior Felix and Alexis Infante, and with youngsters like Jimmy Kelly in the wings, Latin American players promise to have even greater impact on Blue Jay fortunes in the seasons that lie just around the corner. Indeed, the Latin American baseball connection is today alive and well.

Best known for his defensive range at shortstop and his clutch hitting, Tony Fernandez has battled injuries in recent seasons to remain the premier all-around shortstop in all of baseball. The first Blue Jay to garner 200 hits in a season, and holder of the highest single-season BA (.322 in 1987) among regulars, Tony Fernandez set an American League standard for errorless games at his position during the 1989 season.

7. Cold Starts and Colder Finishes on the Shores of Lake Ontario

Below: *Jimy Williams poses with his new uniform sweater at the news conference announcing his somewhat surprising selection as Toronto's fourth manager. The date was October 25, 1985, nine days after the Jays had been eliminated from their first ALCS. Quite ironically, Williams' new uniform number foreshadows the total number of seasons he himself would be able to hold onto the job.*

By spring training camp of 1986 the defending American League Eastern Division Champions had seemingly arrived at a crucial crossroads in their franchise history. Were these upstart no-names who represented Canada's second major league city serious baseball contenders? Or had Toronto's lovable Jays arisen so suddenly to the heights of pennant contention through some kind of an inexplicable fluke? Would they soon fall again in the rapid ebb and flow of shifting team fortunes that has distinguished baseball since the onset of free agency? Or had Pat Gillick's ball club become a true dominant force in the American League East, the showcase product of expert long-range planning by a front office management team that had seemed to do almost everything right from the very outset in 1977? The tentative answer revealed by subsequent 1987 and 1988 seasons seems, of course, to suggest that perhaps it was a little of both.

For starters, a tenth-anniversary season in 1986 was much anticipated far and wide as the Blue Jays' inevitable glory year, but it didn't quite work out that way. Overconfidence perhaps, a slow-start to be sure – these were the factors which conspired to reaffirm that old baseball adage that it is always far easier to win a pennant than it ever is to defend one. Under the reign of new manager Jimy Williams the talented Jays did muster an impressive late-season finish in 1986 that left them nine and a half games back and in fourth place at season's end. The 1986 Blue Jay team was one that simply wouldn't die; in the words of popular baseball analyst Bill James, they were "harder to kill than Rasputin" and a team that eventually had to be given much hard-earned admiration for fighting their way back into the pennant race after an April-May start that left the bullpen in a shambles and pennant hopes buried by an avalanche of early season disasters. By the end of May the ledger stood at 20-26 (11 games behind the Red Sox and last in the division), confidence was shaken in rookie manager Jimy Williams, ace Dave Stieb was floundering with an 0-6 record and 6.83 ERA, and controversy raged over the team's lack of a consistent lead-off hitter. When the Red Sox stumbled badly in July the Jays edged back into the pennant fight, and a nine-game Toronto winning streak at the end of August made it a two-team race and cut the Boston lead to three and a half games on September 1st. In the end it was the Red Sox who caught fire and blew open the division race. The Jays did not fold in September as much as the Red Sox proved invincible, launching their own 11-game unbeaten string in the crucial first weeks of September. Toronto faded only after the race was well settled, slipping finally to fourth place in the first days of October, a whisker behind Detroit and the Yankees in the final season ledger.

At best 1986 was to be remembered as a season of individual milestones, with Clancy and Stieb becoming the club's first

two career 100-game winners, and with George Bell (31 homers and a club-record 108 RBIs) and Jesse Barfield (a club-record 40 homers and 108 RBIs as well) emerging as true major American League batting stars. The play of Bell (who also smacked 38 doubles) and Barfield (with 107 runs scored and a .559 slugging percentage) – along with the inspired if often inconsistent play of Lloyd Moseby (21 homers and 86 RBIs, but a sagging .253 BA and 122 strikeouts) – led even Bill James to speculate on ranking the Toronto outfield among the greatest in baseball history.

James favorably compared the composite offensive statistics of the Blue Jay trio (an average of 31 homers, 101 RBIs, and .284 BA for 1986) with those of such potent outfield combos as the Yankees in the late 1920s (Bob Meusel, Earle Combs and Babe Ruth), the St. Louis Browns in the early 1920s (Baby Doll Jacobson, Jack Tobin and Ken Williams), the Pirates of the late 1960s (Willie Stargell, Matty Alou and Roberto Clemente), and the Yankees of the late 1940s (Charlie Keller, Joe DiMaggio and Tommy Henrich). Yet batting statistics alone do not win pennants, and as James was quick to note, such vaunted offensive outfields as those of the 1966 Pittsburgh Pirates or the 1924 and 1925 St. Louis Browns never translated into a very good win-loss percentage for the team as a whole. If 1986 was the ultimate year of the great Toronto offensive outfield, it was also a most disappointing season for Blue Jays

Above: *Kelly Gruber slides safely into second with a stolen base against the Red Sox while Boston's shortstop Spike Owen awaits a tardy throw. Gruber stole 23 bases in 1988, while being caught only 5 times.*

fans primed for a pennant and hopeful of a return to post-season play.

When it comes to labelling baseball summers in terms of highlight individual performances, 1987, in turn, was indisputably the "Year of George Bell" – unless it was more fittingly labelled the "Year of the Ultimate Collapse." Ironically, Bell's season-long successes and the team's final-week failures were intricately woven together as Bell's MVP season tailed off into a final-week slump that many blamed in part for the seven-game season-ending slide that handed another division pennant to Detroit. Yet in the end it was as much the crucial season-ending injuries to shortstop Tony Fernandez (taken out on a rough slide by Detroit's Bill Madlock in the season's penultimate week) and catcher Ernie Whitt (a bruised hand) during the final dramatic 10 days of September, as it was the hitting slump of Bell, that explained the Jays' inability to pull off a single victory in the final three-game set at Detroit. What was almost lost in the final week of pennant disappointment was the indelible impression that this 1987 Toronto ball club was indeed a beautiful team to watch, and the season's final two tightly-contested series with Detroit (three wins and one loss at home the final week of September, and three crucial defeats at Detroit the following weekend) provided some of the most colorful and dramatic baseball in the long annals of American League championship season play.

Perhaps the most painful irony of Toronto's brief baseball history is that the Jays played far better baseball in those final seven games (three at home with Milwau-

Above: *Jesse Barfield waves to the Toronto crowd after hitting his 40th home run during the 1986 season. Barfield, who led the league that year, thus became the first Blue Jay to reach the 40-homer plateau.*

Right: *Tom Henke was originally selected from the Rangers in compensation for the loss of free agent Cliff Johnson, and the fireballer from Missouri soon emerged as one of the finest short relievers in the game today.*

kee and the final three-game set at Detroit) that they lost than did the four division champions (Detroit, Minnesota, St. Louis and Los Angeles) in any of the 1987 post-season games which were to follow. But first impressions and the hindsight of memory are often as illusionary in baseball as they are in all other walks of life. The Jays did not exactly collapse in the season's final month; they simply could not win the crucial close games due to impotent hitting down the stretch (only three Blue Jays hit higher than .222 during the final week of the season), which neutralized strong pitching to the very end. Nor did Toronto lead the division for much of the season, trailing the Yankees and Brewers as well as the Tigers for much of the summer and standing at only 14 games over .500 near the end of July. It was in August and September that the lethal Toronto bats boomed at a torrid pace and the club played nearly .700 ball for much of the final two months; yet Toronto still trailed Detroit by a full game on September 1st. The Tigers were again in first place on September 17th, and it was only after sweeping three of four from Detroit on the last days of September that the Blue Jays seemed to take temporary command of the race. Yet in the end the Toronto ball club could not avoid what it had so successfully avoided all season long – a prolonged losing slump. The ultimate irony about the 1987 Blue Jays, when all was said and done, was that they could not win the close, well-pitched games which their team speed and strong starting pitching should have equipped them to win. In slugfests (games with more than 10 runs scored) the Jays were ironically the most successful team in either league, winning 37 and dropping only 17(.685 percentage). In pitcher's duels, however, the Jays' winning percentage dropped to an anemic .417(17-24), easily one of the year's worst marks in either league.

The late-season failures of 1987 were abated only by the high expectations for 1988. Could the Blue Jays rebound? Was this finally to be the year of Toronto's first World Series? After all, the outfield of Bell, Barfield and Moseby was still intact and potent, and the lively young arms of Stieb, Clancy and Key were still the envy of the league. And despite the stability of the Blue Jays' roster (only 14 regular starters at the eight defensive positions over the past five seasons), this was a team featuring only one key player (Ernie Whitt) over the age of 31. Everyone's pre-season pick this time around seemed to be the ill-fated yet multi-talented Jays. Sparky Anderson's Detroit Tigers now seemed over-aged, and no other serious challenger seemed quite equal to the task of derailing a Toronto team that seemed capable of pacing the league in almost all offensive and defensive categories.

But as 1985 was followed by the slow start of 1986, so 1987's final disastrous week was encored by an even slower start in April 1988. From the first days of spring training there were ominous signs as MVP George Bell feuded loudly with field boss Jimy Williams over his assigned role as permanent DH, a move calculated to

Top left: *Jim Clancy winds up for the pitch. Enjoying a 12-year career in Toronto, which produced a 128-140 record, Clancy's departure to free agency in 1989 left Ernie Whitt as the only remaining original Blue Jay.*

Bottom left: *Jesse Barfield enjoyed superb power seasons in 1985-87, slugging 95 homers and knocking home 276 runs over this stretch of his career. Barfield was also the league leader in assists among outfielders in each of these seasons – a testimony to the quality of his all-around offensive and defensive play.*

mid-season incident in Minnesota, where Bell was yanked from the lineup after two badly misplayed outfield balls, seemed to capsulate the star's year of frustration, one which saw him eclipse Rick Bosetti's 1979 club standard for outfield errors.

George Bell did come on strong offensively at season's end and the Jays did finish with a sudden flurry, with six wins in a row, nine victories in the final 10 games, and 15 wins over the final 18 contests. For the last three weeks of September Toronto was once again recognizably the best team in baseball, coming from eight and a half games off the pace on September 20th to a scant two games out after the final day's play. But seasons are played out over the long summer months, and Toronto's inspired late-season heroics were once again far too little and altogether too late.

Bell's persistent sulking was not the only sign of dissension on the troubled 1988 club, however. A contingent of the team's dedicated Christian athletes, led by group spokesmen Jesse Barfield and Tony Fernandez, fumed over manager Williams' early-season suspension of road-trip clubhouse chapel sessions. Religion had always been as familiar as stray towels in the Jays' clubhouse, yet Williams saw the practice as disruptive of the club's normal baseball routine. When club officials balked as well at the idea of Fernandez and teammate Kelly Gruber wearing team-logo caps and jackets while promoting a religious fund raiser for starving third-world children, morale among activist Christian players

Above: *Selected from the Red Sox organization in the 1976 AL expansion draft, Ernie Whitt today remains the single original Blue Jay.*

Right: *George Bell follows the flight of the ball after smashing another homer.*

Opposite: *Dave Stieb is captured releasing his patented fastball.*

advance promising rookie speedsters Sil Campusano and Rob Ducey into the Toronto outfield and strengthen the club measurably on the defensive front. While Campusano and Ducey had already ingloriously played their way back to Syracuse by opening day, however, malcontents Bell and Moseby were again entrenched in the Toronto outfield when the new season opened on the road in Kansas City. Bell promptly answered his critics by clouting three mammoth homers on opening day at Royals Stadium, but then just as promptly tumbled into a season-long slump from which he inevitably emerged as the singular goat in a season of lost opportunities. A

410

dipped still further. Williams managerial tenure seemed in considerable jeopardy, in light of such dissension piled atop the ongoing feud with Bell, but at season's end front office management made it abundantly clear just where it stood in regard to the beleaguered manager and his unhappy players. The 45-year-old Jimy Williams was rehired in October, while George Bell remained the favored subject of continued trade rumors throughout much of the off-season. After all, blame for the poor showing of 1988 might easily be attributed as much to repeated injuries – this time to Tony Fernandez (again) and Jimmy Key (who missed 13 starts due to minor arm surgery) and to the uncooperativeness of Bell and Moseby – as to any leadership flaws of the taciturn Williams. That the Blue Jays finished 1988 by winning the final six games of the season, closing to within two games of division champion Boston, may also have had much to do with rescuing the controversial manager at the bitter conclusion of a second consecutive disappointing campaign.

Another major story of 1988 was veteran All-Star hurler Dave Stieb. Stieb, along with stellar fireballing reliever Tom Henke, seemed at times to be misused by dugout and front office management. Both pitchers were known to have contract clauses specifying bonus payments attached to innings pitched, and both appeared not to receive their fair share of pitching workload in what all-too-often seemed a calculated front-office conspiracy to sabotage such bonus agreements. But whatever his motives for discontent, Stieb fought back with a banner season (16-8, 3.04 ERA), capped by two brilliant year-end mound performances that highlighted Toronto's otherwise disappointing season. On September 11th, before a sparse night crowd at Cleveland, the 31-year-old right-hander came within a single pitch of achieving a first franchise no-hitter. A two-strike, two-out bad hop single off the bat of Julio Franco in cavernous Municipal Stadium ruined Stieb's initial bid for baseball immortality. A mere six days later, this time at home against Baltimore, pinch-hitter Jim Traber blooped a fatal two-out ninth-inning single into right field to erase Stieb's second consecutive near-no-hit effort. While Dave Stieb thus became baseball's first pitcher ever to miss back-to-back no-hitters, each time on the potential final pitch, Toronto remained the only major league franchise never to enjoy a hometown hurler's no-hit effort. But there was a small consolation at least in Stieb's brilliant accomplishment itself – perhaps the best single back-to-back pitching performance

since Johnny Vander Meer successfully realized two consecutive no-hitters for the Cincinnati Reds way back in 1938.

Bill James seemingly put it best. On September 20, 1987, the Toronto Blue Jays began a fateful seven-game home and away series that mercilessly ended the 1987 season and saw the Jays unable to win even a single game which would have brought home a second division pennant. On that day the Jays still had a clean baseball slate,

and yet they never would again enjoy such a luxurious reprieve from the harsh judgments of baseball history. For with that final seven-game collapse against Detroit an era as well as a season dramatically ended, and the Blue Jays of 1987 passed into the history books, alongside the 1964 Philadelphia Phillies, as authors of baseball's most memorable late-season collapse. Whatever the team had accomplished during its first decade had always been deliciously unanticipated; it always exceeded all reasonable expectations. After the dramatic late-season fold-up of September 1987, however, the team seemed to enter that true fellowship of major league franchises owning an indelible baseball history – a history of excruciating failure, of yearly frustration and inexcusable annual loss under the most inopportune of circumstances. Like the Cubs and Red Sox and Phillies, the Blue Jays would forevermore

History is made in 1987 as Jimmy Key launches a first pitch of the season to Cleveland's Tony Bernazard, and for the first time in major league history the baseball season begins outside of the United States.

BLUE JAYS

seem doomed to lose the big one, the single game needed for pennant or World Championship. Although barely a decade old, this was now a franchise with a tradition of failure cast in the same mold as some of baseball's most lovable and battle-worn franchises – the Brooklyn Dodgers of the early 1950s, the Detroit Tigers throughout the 1960s, the Cubs and Red Sox of the past four decades, or the Phillies and White Sox of the entire past half-century. The future and the past would always be measured differently after that season-ending seven-game confrontation with the Tigers. For it was precisely then that the Jays and their fans had reached the brink for the first time and had for the first time as well been turned back in utter and unpardonable defeat.

But as baseball seasons are long and each fresh spring brings renewed pennant dreams, the agony of defeat fades quickly, even if it returns regularly and with nagging persistence. Thus the bitter final week of 1987 and the failure to get off the ground running for 1988 were both eventually swept away in the late euphoria of the action-packed 1989 season. At least the second half of the 1989 season, for at its outset, 1989 seemed destined to be merely another tired replay of 1986 and 1988. George Bell was still pouting about frequent if not daily DH duties. The bullpen was again in disarray as Mark Eichhorn faltered in spring training and was dealt to Atlanta, while Tom Henke proved unproductive in early going and sank from his expected role as the traditional closer. Longtime standby Jesse Barfield was traded away in April to the Yankees for promising left-hander Al Leiter, but Leiter was damaged goods who spent the bulk of the season wasted on the disabled list. It was an inauspicious start indeed, and by mid-May the floundering Jays were buried in last place with Detroit, already five and a half games off the pace of the mediocre Red Sox, themselves only playing at a .500 pace. Only the ineptitude of the remainder of the league's Eastern Division kept the Jays from falling completely from sight during the earliest weeks of the 1989 campaign.

The embattled Jimy Williams seemingly had little respect from his disgruntled players from the earliest days of spring training, and Toronto newspapers were speculating on a managerial change almost from before opening day. One of the few highlights was the early season appearance of rookie Junior Felix, a 24-year-old Dominican outfielder with only three seasons of professional baseball experience. Felix poked a homer in his first big-league at-bat – on the first pitch served in his May 4th debut against the California Angels in Exhibition Stadium – in the process becoming only the eleventh man in league history to accomplish this rare feat. Another early highlight was the hitting display of Kelly Gruber on April 16th. In the season's third home game against Kansas City the popular Toronto third baseman became the first batsman in team history to hit for the cycle, stroking a single, double, triple and homer within a single game. But while Gruber continued to hit early, maintaining a .300-plus average on into July, and Felix offered to salvage the botched Barfield trade, little else seemed to go right for the Jays throughout April or the earliest weeks of May.

The true turning point of the Jay's thirteenth season came in mid-May, in fact, with the involuntary departure of Jimy Williams and the arrival of new skipper Cito Gaston, the fifth in club history. Williams had long since worn out his welcome with the usually patient Toronto fans and certainly with his own players, and the club stood at 12-24, mired in sixth place at the time of his firing. But dismissal of Williams on May 15th seemed at least temporarily to throw the organization into even further chaos. No clear managerial replacement immediately emerged, which bought acting skipper Cito Gaston time to get the Jays off and running once again. Ex-Yankee skipper Lou Piniella was mentioned prominently in the press, as was Bob Bailor, now manager of the Jays' Triple-A club in Syracuse. But Piniella was not freed from his existing contract as advisor to Yankees owner George Steinbrenner and

Opposite: *Kelly Gruber follows through on a base hit, one of 158 he collected in 1988. Gruber has supplemented fine fielding at third base with increased offensive production over the past two seasons, batting over .300 for much of the 1989 campaign before slipping to a respectable career-high season BA of .290.*

Below: *Cito Gaston became the Blue Jays' fifth manager on an interim basis in May of 1989, leading the club to a dramatic reversal of form throughout the remainder of the season, and to a second division title as well.*

Above: *Tony Fernandez hits from both sides of the plate with authority, adding to his threat to opposing pitchers. In his exceptional 1987 season, Fernandez hit .297 from the right side and .334 as a lefty. While George Bell bested Alan Trammell of Detroit that year for league MVP honors, many Toronto watchers contend that Bell was not even the most valuable player on his own team – that honor may well have belonged to Tony Fernandez.*

was thus unavailable for serious consideration, despite his rumored favored status in the eyes of top executive Pat Gillick. In the end it was the 45-year-old batting coach Gaston who was tendered the permanent job, thus becoming baseball's third-ever black field boss. Gaston had taken over a spluttering flock but soon had them moving forward again with renewed dedication to the American League pennant chase. Under Gaston the Jays were to play at a torrid .611 pace (77-49) throughout the remaining months of the campaign. The middle of the season seemed one doomed to a desperate chase of the high-flying Orioles, however, and an exciting two-team pennant race was the scenario on tap for the final weeks of American League eastern divisional play.

It was in early August that the Jays finally moved into command of the American League East, a division waiting for someone to make a move as six teams sputtered behind overachieving Baltimore throughout most of the summer. Dave Stieb's third near no-hitter in slightly less than a year – this time a near-flawless masterpiece which fell just one pitch short of a thirteenth big-league regular-season perfect game – was a turning point against the Yankees on August 4th in Toronto. This time it was rookie Roberto Kelly of New York who slapped a double to left on a 2-0 count with two down in the ninth, making hard-luck Dave Stieb the fifth pitcher of 1989 to lose a no-hitter in the ninth inning. The game was the twenty-eighth played in the new SkyDome and was witnessed by a then-record Toronto crowd of 48,789.

If Gaston's elevation as manager had been a crucial change, another personnel move in early August was perhaps equally as crucial to the Jays' ultimate pennant chances. Just before the August 1st trading deadline, Jeff Musselman was shipped off to the National League New York Mets for veteran speedster Mookie Wilson, while a day later reserve veteran outfielder Lee Mazzilli was claimed off waivers from the self-same Mets. The popular Mookie Wilson became an instantaneous on-field leader with his hustle and experienced outfield glove play, while Lee Mazzilli provided a needed late-season clubhouse leader and part-time DH and pinch hitter as well. The two expatriated New York ball-players were such instant hits with the overjoyed Toronto ballpark faithful that they quickly received the widespread joint nickname of "Mazzookie."

The season ultimately came down to a final weekend series, a true fan's delight fortuitously provided by the omniscient schedule maker. The Jays had been unable to pull away from Frank Robinson's inspired young Orioles, despite a torrid August streak which brought them from five games arrears to first place before Labor Day, and Baltimore was still but a single game behind when the final three-game set was launched in the SkyDome on September 29th. The first few innings of the tense series opener seemed to foreshadow a replay of 1987, as the Jays performed listlessly and wasted several golden scoring opportunities. But luck and spunk was with the Blue Jays in 1989, and an eighth-inning mistake by Baltimore hurler Gregg Olsen was the window of opportunity that Cito Gaston's club sought. Olsen wild pitched home the game-tying run in the eighth, and reliever Mark Williamson yielded a game-winning single to Lloyd Moseby in the eleventh to spark a come-from-behind, 2-1, extra-inning victory. Friday's thrilling win was matched by similar heroics in the late innings of Saturday's game. Williamson

Mookie Wilson watches the flight of an infield fly ball. Acquired from the New York Mets in 1989 for Jeff Musselman, the speedy outfielder became an instant hit with Toronto fans.

was again touched up for the tying and winning runs in a three-run eighth inning rally which preserved a 4-3 pennant-clinch victory. Aided by Mookie Wilson's and Fred McGriff's run-producing singles and George Bell's vital game-clinching sacrifice fly, Toronto had clinched their second division crown in half a decade. But this time it was the one that had so cruelly eluded them for three successive seasons, each one marked by late-September failures and each crammed with mid-season disappointment and a faltering team self-image.

One reason for the Jays' successes in 1989 had to be the dramatic re-emergence of George Bell. Where Bell had failed down the stretch during his earlier controversial MVP year, in 1989 he unarguably carried the club when the chips were down and the pennant was on the line during late August and September play. No longer swinging exclusively for the fences, nor faltering

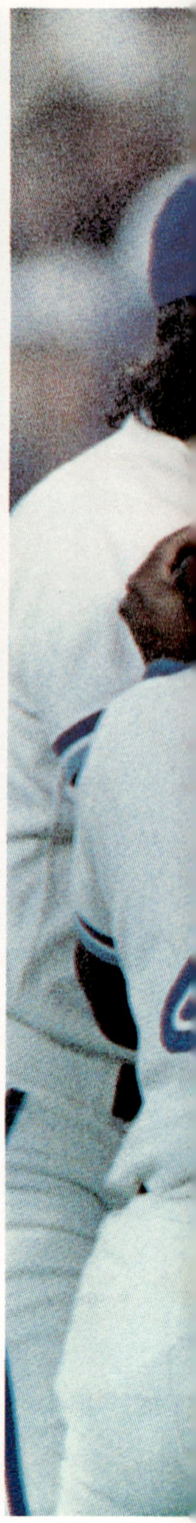

Right: *A joyous clubhouse celebration begins as Nelson Liriano (left) is congratulated by Mookie Wilson after batting home two runs in the 13th frame to give the Blue Jays a key come-from-behind 6-5 win over the Boston Red Sox during the late-season 1989 stretch run.*

Far right: *Batting star Lloyd Moseby is hugged by the shouting Tony Fernandez (second from right) after driving home the crucial run against Baltimore that clinched a division title on September 29, 1989. The other identifiable players are Manny Lee (number 4), Rob Ducey (top left), Ernie Whitt (hat reversed), and pitcher Tom Henke (far right).*

with runners in scoring position, Bell slugged away relentlessly throughout the later summer, compiling his most impressive offensive numbers since the glory year of 1987 – 18 HRs, 88 Runs, 104 RBIs, .297 BA. In a summer when other contenders lacked a true offensive leader – Canseco missed much of the season for Oakland, Cal Ripken hit only .257 (with 21 HRs and 93 RBIs) for Baltimore, and Minnesota's Kirbie Puckett wasted a superb offensive year on a non-contending team – Bell once again seemed a legitimate candidate by year's end to capture his second league MVP Award in three seasons.

The excitement of a second pennant season in Toronto was matched throughout the final months of the summer by the hoopla surrounding baseball's newest and most luxurious stadium. For the first time modern technology could provide a combination of baseball's natural venue of outdoor play with defense against the elements and with all the creature comforts of foul-weather indoor play. At the cost of an additional $80 million (Canadian dollars), the prototype Toronto SkyDome boasted a moveable roof which covered 53,000 plush baseball seats in a matter of one half-hour or less when bad weather descended upon downtown Toronto. Unlike previous domed stadiums, this one was neither a baseball disaster nor a financial albatross. SkyDome management and Blue Jays officials projected shortly before opening night that the new dome would generate a cash flow of over $20 million for 55 home playing dates with the first partial season. Unlike the Louisiana Superdome, for example, which still loses almost $6 million (US dollars) yearly in operating expenses, Toronto's new baseball showpiece seemed guaranteed to make money from the day it opened, only partially completed, in early June. And the Jays themselves found their new surroundings conducive to inspired play as well, playing almost unbeatable baseball there the final month of the season and

compiling a 12-0 mark in the first season's play during those games in which the Skydome roof remained closed to the outside elements.

By season's end the Blue Jays had finally rid themselves – at least temporarily – of the nagging loser-image that had marked the second phase of their brief franchise history. Around the corner were the powerful Oakland Athletics who had cruised through the West Division with 99 victories and boasted the best pitching staff in baseball. Paced by Dave Stewart (21-9), Mike Moore (19-11) and Storm Davis (19-7) – as well as the league's top closer in veteran Dennis Eckersley – Manager Tony LaRussa's Athletics were a formidable final obstacle to a first-ever World Series appearance for Canada's beloved Blue Jays. But much had already been established by the conclusion of the topsy-turvy 1989 season, as the Toronto Blue Jays were finally a team that had reasonably lived up to preseason hype and fan expectations. What now remained to be written was simply the dramatic and as yet unforeseen last chapter in one of baseball's most successful expansion-era stories.

It was a different kind of Toronto team that entered the 1989 ALCS, not at all like the euphoric but inexperienced bunch that had bolted from the gate and then as quickly folded up against Kansas City in the 1985 post-season series. This was a team that blended raw youth with considerable experience. Bell, Moseby, Stieb, Key, Gruber, Fernandez, Whitt – all were veterans of several tense seasons of trying to shake the dogged image of last-minute losers. Now a plateau had been reached and a burden had been lifted. This was a team for whom the pressure was seemingly off and World Series play would be the unexpected icing to a fine comeback season. It was a good thing, also, that expectations were not too high, for the Jays had little chance against the pennant-hungry Athletics who outmanned them at nearly every position.

Nelson Liriano ducks back safely to first as Mark McGwire awaits a pick-off throw during SkyDome action in the third game of the 1989 ALCS. Baserunners were scarce throughout the series for Toronto, and productive hitting with runners in scoring position proved to be even a scarcer commodity for Cito Gaston's out-manned team.

This was a truly awesome Oakland team that entered post-season play. Featured was the best pitching staff in baseball, including four of the season's top winners and two of baseball's most underrated pitchers. Dave Stewart (21-9) had led all big-league hurlers in wins over the past three summers, despite his inability to capture Cy Young homers. Mike Moore (19-11) had labored in almost total obscurity in Seattle for several seasons before 1989 provided him with a luxurious opportunity to prove his talents with a winning team. Dennis Eckersley was still among the best short-relievers in baseball. Add to this the speed and daring of Rickey Henderson on the basepaths and the power of Mark McGwire and Jose Canseco (the only two men in baseball history to hit over 30 homers in each of their first three big-league seasons) and you had a team reminiscent of the late 1970s Yankees or the slugging 1950s Dodgers. This Oakland team was, to make matters worse, a team driven by a fevered mission. Having been embarrassed in 1988 post-season play by the underdog Dodgers, Tony LaRussa's men were this year determined to obtain their rightful spot in the history books among baseball's strongest all-time teams.

In game one, at Oakland, it was Stieb vs. Stewart. The Athetics' Rickey Henderson broke up a potential double play with a hard slide into Blue Jay second baseman Nelson Liriano in the sixth inning, sparking Oakland's game-winning rally in a come-from-behind victory against Toronto's ill-fated starter. The final tally was 7-3. The second day of series play started out on what appeared to be an ominous note for Oakland. Bothered with a migraine headache, slugger Jose Canseco had to be scratched from the starting lineup, and made only a brief, late-inning appearance. But the absence of Canseco seemed to make little difference as Rickey Henderson took up where he left off in game one, stroking two hits, stealing two bases, and scoring two runs as Oakland jumped out to a 6-1 lead before Toronto's futile and insufficient late-inning rally. The Jays could come up with only two more runs, dropping the game 6-3.

Game three provided the one evening of true hometown excitement alotted to Toronto fans in the series, as Jimmy Key held the Oakland bats in check and the Jays rallied for four runs in the fourth and three more in the seventh, sweeping to a much-needed victory in the inaugural game of SkyDome post-season play. Tony Fernandez keyed both Toronto big innings with a pair of clutch doubles as the Jays reached 19-game winner Storm Davis (19-7) early and put an end to any thoughts of a short-lived Oakland sweep. Rickey Henderson was not exactly quiet in this game, scoring twice and stealing his record seventh series base as the fired-up Athletics took an early 3-0 lead. Yet Jimmy Key survived a shaky start and held on to win, scattering seven hits over six innings before giving way to Jim Acker and Tom Henke, who together held Oakland at bay.

Although the Blue Jays had plenty of chances in game four – leaving the potential tying runs on base in both the third and eighth innings – ultimately it was the heavy-hitting A's who ruled the field. Behind Rickey Henderson's pair of two-run homers, and a Canseco homer, the A's disappointed SkyDome fans to the tune of 6-5. In the fifth and final game Oakland's Dave Stewart once more outdueled Dave Stieb. Toronto fans had something to shout about when Moseby stroked a bases-empty homer in the eighth and George Bell followed suit in the ninth, but it was all too little and too late, as fire-balling Dennis Eckersley again closed the door in the ninth. The Athletics were on their way to a World Series against the cross-bay rival San Francisco Giants.

In the end it had simply been too much of Rickey Henderson and too much of Dennis Eckersley. The Jays had played gamely if not well; the dormant bats which plagued Toronto throughout the series may just as well have been attributed to the strength of Oakland pitching as to any lack of championship effort on the part of Toronto hitters. But the ultimate irony that surrounded this series was perhaps that the Athletics won on pitching and dominant team speed, and not merely on the potent bats of their awesome sluggers. It was the enthusiastic Rickey Henderson who walked away with the Series' MVP Award, as well as with his long-awaited ticket to the World Series. But for Blue Jay fans and players a trip to the World Series would have to wait at least one more long baseball year.

George Bell here makes contact with a pitch during game four of the 1989 ALCS. Bell slugged the ball consistently down the late-season stretch, yet his bat – along with those of his teammates – was effectively silenced by strong Oakland pitching throughout the short-lived playoff series.

Blue Jays Achievements

YEAR-BY-YEAR BLUE JAYS STANDINGS AND TEAM LEADERS

Year	Position	Record	Margin	Manager	Batting		Pitching Leader		
1977	7	54-107	45½	Hartsfield	Howell	.316	Lemanczyk	13-16	4.25 ERA
1978	7	59-102	40	Hartsfield	Howell	.270	Clancy	10-12	4.09 ERA
1979	7	53-109	50½	Hartsfield	Griffin	.287	Underwood	9-16	3.69 ERA
1980	7	67-95	36	Mattick	Woods	.300	Clancy	13-16	3.30 ERA
1981	7	16-42	19	Mattick	D. Garcia	.252	Stieb	11-10	3.19 ERA
	7	21-27	7½	*(Second Half of Split-Season due to Players' Union Strike)*					
1981*	7	37-69		**Split Season Totals*					
1982	6	78-84	17	Cox	D. Garcia	.310	Stieb	17-14	3.25 ERA
1983	4	89-73	9	Cox	Moseby	.315	Stieb	17-12	3.04 ERA
1984	2	89-73	15	Cox	Collins	.308	Alexander	17-6	3.13 ERA
1985	1	99-62	+ 2	Cox	Mulliniks	.295	Alexander	17-10	3.45 ERA
1986	4	86-76	9½	Williams	Fernandez	.310	Eichhorn	14-6	1.72 ERA
1987	2	96-66	2	Williams	Fernandez	.322	Key	17-8	2.76 ERA
1988	3	87-75	2	Williams	Mulliniks	.300	Stieb	16-8	3.04 ERA
1989	1	89-73	+ 2	Williams/ Gaston	Bell	.297	Stieb	17-8	3.35 ERA

SINGLE-SEASON BLUE JAYS PITCHING RECORDS

ERA (150 Innings)	Dave Stieb	2.48	1985
ERA (100 Innings)	Mark Eichhorn	1.72	1986
Wins	Dave Stieb	17	1982
	Dave Stieb	17	1983
	Dave Stieb	17	1989
	Doyle Alexander	17	1984
	Doyle Alexander	17	1985
	Jimmy Key	17	1987
Losses	Jerry Garvin	18	1977
	Phil Huffman	18	1979
Winning Pct (10 decisions)	Doyle Alexander	.739	1984
Strikeouts	Dave Stieb	198	1984
Walks	Jim Clancy	128	1980
Saves	Tom Henke	34	1987
Games	Mark Eichhorn	89	1987
Complete Games	Dave Stieb	19	1982
Games Started	Jim Clancy	40	1982
Shutouts	Dave Stieb	5	1982
Innings Pitched	Dave Stieb	288.1	1982
Home Runs Allowed	Jerry Garvin	33	1977
Consecutive Games Won	Dennis Lamp	11	1985
Consecutive Games Lost	Jerry Garvin	10	1977
	Paul Mirabella	10	1980
Consecutive Games Lost (2 seasons)	Tom Underwood	13	1978, 1979
Consecutive Complete Games	Dave Stieb	7	1980
Wild Pitches	Dave Lemanczyk	20	1977
Balks	Jimmy Key	5	1987

SINGLE-SEASON BLUE JAYS BATTING RECORDS

Batting Average (350 ABs)	Tony Fernandez	.322	1987
Batting Average (100 Games)	Rance Mulliniks	.324	1984
Home Runs	George Bell	47	1987
Home Runs (Left-Handed)	Fred McGriff	36	1989
Runs Batted In	George Bell	134	1987
Hits	Tony Fernandez	213	1986
Singles	Tony Fernandez	161	1986
Doubles	Tony Fernandez	41	1988
Triples	Alfredo Griffin	15	1980
	Dave Collins	15	1984
	Lloyd Moseby	15	1984
Slugging Percentage	George Bell	.605	1987
Extra-Base Hits	George Bell	83	1987
Game-Winning RBIs	George Bell	16	1987
Sacrifices	Luis Gomez	22	1978
Stolen Bases	Dave Collins	60	1984
	Cliff Johnson	60	1984
Pinch Hits	Wayne Nordhagen	11	1982
Strikeouts	Fred McGriff	149	1988
Total Bases	George Bell	369	1987
Hitting Streak	George Bell	22	1989
Grand Slam Home Runs	George Bell	2	1985, 1987
	Roy Howell	2	1979
On-Base Percentage	Cliff Johnson	.393	1984
Hit-by-Pitch	Damaso Garcia	9	1984
Hitting for the Cycle	Kelly Gruber	1	1989
Games	Tony Fernandez	163	1986

ALL-TIME BLUE JAYS CAREER BATTING LEADERS

Games Played	Lloyd Moseby	1392
At Bats	Lloyd Moseby	5124
Runs Scored	Lloyd Moseby	768
Hits	Lloyd Moseby	1319
Batting Average	George Bell	.297
Home Runs	George Bell	181
Run Batted In	George Bell	654
Stolen Bases	Lloyd Moseby	255
Sacrifice Hits	Alfredo Griffin	67
Strikeouts	Lloyd Moseby	1015

ALL-TIME BLUE JAYS CAREER PITCHING LEADERS

Innings Pitched	Dave Stieb	2458
Earned Run Average	Jimmy Key	3.36
Wins	Dave Stieb	148
Losses	Jim Clancy	140
Winning Percentage	Doyle Alexander	.639
Strikeouts	Dave Stieb	1432
Walks	Dave Stieb	873
Games	Dave Stieb	357
Shutouts	Dave Stieb	28
Saves	Tom Henke	122
Games Started	Dave Stieb	349
Complete Games	Dave Stieb	99
Hit Batsmen	Dave Stieb	110
Wild Pitches	Jim Clancy	82

BLUE JAYS POST-SEASON RECORD

Playoffs

Year	*Opponent*	*Wins-Losses*
1985	Kansas City Royals	2-3
1989	Oakland Athletics	1-4

BLUE JAYS LEAGUE LEADERS AND AWARD WINNERS

1979	Alfredo Griffin	Rookie of the Year
1985	Dave Stieb	ERA Champion (2.48)
1987	George Bell	Most Valuable Player
1989	Fred McGriff	Home Run Leader (36)

Right: *Jim Gott, Blue Jays right-hander, winds up for the pitch.*

Index

Numbers in *italics* indicate illustrations